D0850753

IN THE MORNING

WHEN I RISE

*Life-Giving Conversations
with God*

KATHERINE J. BUTLER

AMY E. MASON

RONALD A. BEERS

Tyndale House Publishers, Inc.
Carol Stream, Illinois

LIVING EXPRESSIONS COLLECTION

Living Expressions invites you to explore God's Word and express your creativity in ways that are refreshing to the spirit and restorative to the soul.

Visit Tyndale online at www.tyndale.com.

TYNDALE, Tyndale's quill logo, *Living Expressions*, and the Living Expressions logo are registered trademarks of Tyndale House Publishers, Inc.

In the Morning When I Rise: Life-Giving Conversations with God

Copyright © 2020 by Ronald A. Beers. All rights reserved.

Cover photograph of mountains copyright © elgad/Depositphotos.com. All rights reserved.

Cover photograph of sunrise copyright © valio84sl/Depositphotos.com. All rights reserved.

Cover photograph of birds copyright © Ingimage/Deposiphotoscom. All rights reserved.

Designed by Ron C. Kaufmann

Scripture quotations are adapted from the *Holy Bible*, New Living Translation, copyright © 1996, 2004, 2015 by Tyndale House Foundation. Used by permission of Tyndale House Publishers, Inc., Carol Stream, Illinois 60188. All rights reserved.

For information about special discounts for bulk purchases, please contact Tyndale House Publishers at csresponse@tyndale.com, or call 1-800-323-9400.

ISBN 978-1-4964-4215-4

Printed in China

26   25   24   23   22   21   20
7   6   5   4   3   2   1

INTRODUCTION

DO YOU LONG TO HEAR God's voice more clearly? Do you wish he would speak into your current situation? It can be tempting to believe that God is silent about the struggles and challenges you face every day. However, nothing could be further from the truth. He wants you to tell him what's on your mind, and he wants to tell you what is on *his* mind. God speaks to us primarily through his Word, the Bible. To hear him, you simply need to take the time to quietly listen—to read his Word and hear him speak through it. This book offers a unique way to help you do that.

In the Morning When I Rise poses many of the questions you may want to ask God. Over the course of one hundred mornings, you are certain to find many questions that you would love to hear God answer. What's wonderful is how God answers each of these questions in his Word.

Each reading begins with two related questions. The answers are drawn directly from the Bible, often using several verses woven together from different parts of Scripture. In some cases, the verses have been slightly paraphrased in voice or tense to keep with the theme of God talking directly to *you*.

God's Word is different and more powerful than any other book ever written. Because the Bible is a living document, conceived and inspired by God himself, it uniquely applies to each person who reads it, and God speaks uniquely to each individual through it—though of course there are also many truths and principles that apply to all people.

After you have spent time listening to God speak, pray the prayer that follows in each daily reading. These prayers are also taken directly from Scripture, and the wording has occasionally been adapted to fit the theme of your response to God. Let these prayers bless, inspire, and motivate you at the beginning of your day.

At the end of each reading, a short devotional thought or exercise will help you apply more deeply what you have read. This is the only part of the day's reading that is not adapted from God's Word.

Here are a few tips to help you get the most out of this devotional:

1. Read *slowly*. God's Word was never meant to be skimmed over. It is deep, rich, and worthy of your attention. Take the time to allow God's words to sink into your heart.

4

2. Read *often*. We encourage you to stay committed to reading God's Word daily, because the more you read it, the more you will learn to recognize God's voice. Learning how to distinguish God's voice from your own, or from the voice of the enemy, has great power in your life.

3. Read *prayerfully*. Each morning, take time to settle into a quiet place, relax, and pray for an open heart as you read God's Word. Ask God to help you set aside distractions so you can be fully present and ready to receive his truth.

God has something to say to you about whatever issues and concerns you are facing. We pray that he will richly bless you as you ask him your questions, read his Word, and learn to recognize his voice.

In Psalm 27:8, God gives us an invitation: "Come and talk with me." May your heart respond as King David's did: "Listen to my voice in the morning, LORD. Each morning I bring my requests to you and wait expectantly" (Psalm 5:3). "Each morning I will sing with joy about your unfailing love. For you have been my refuge, a place of safety when I am in distress" (Psalm 59:16).

HE IS MAKING YOU INTO A NEW PERSON!

Lord, how does believing in you change my life?
Anyone who belongs to me has become a new person.
The old life is gone; a new life has begun! From my
glorious, unlimited resources, I will empower you
with inner strength through the Holy Spirit.

2 CORINTHIANS 5:17; EPHESIANS 3:16

*What does this process of becoming a new
person look like?*
Don't copy the behavior and customs of this world,
but let me transform you into a new person by changing the way you think. Then you will learn to know
my will for you, which is good and pleasing and
perfect.

ROMANS 12:2

What can I pray to truly transform my life?
Since I have heard about you, Jesus, and have learned
the truth that comes from you, help me throw off my

old sinful nature and my former way of life, which is corrupted by lust and deception. Instead, let the Spirit renew my thoughts and attitudes. Help me put on my new nature, created to be like you—truly righteous and holy.

EPHESIANS 4:21-24

Before you came to know Jesus Christ, you operated only in your own strength. When you began a personal relationship with Jesus, you became filled with the Holy Spirit, and the very life and power of God now dwells within you. God uses many avenues to transform your thinking and thus your actions, but you have to be open to his work and surrender to the process of change. Pray the prayer above with your hands open and lifted toward heaven as a symbol of your surrender to God's transforming work in your life.

THE FREEING POWER OF THE RESURRECTION

Lord, why is the resurrection of Jesus essential to my faith?

If there is no resurrection of the dead, then Christ has not been raised. And if Christ has not been raised, then your faith is useless and you are still guilty of your sins. In that case, all who have died believing in Christ are lost! And if your hope in Christ is only for this life, you are more to be pitied than anyone in the world. But in fact, Christ has been raised from the dead.

1 CORINTHIANS 15:16-20

Jesus, how does your resurrection affect me personally?

I am the resurrection and the life. Anyone who believes in me will live, even after dying. Everyone who lives in me and believes in me will never ever die. I died for you so that you who receive my new life will no longer live for yourself. Instead, you will live for me, who died and was raised for you.

JOHN 11:25-26; 2 CORINTHIANS 5:15

What prayer will help me affirm my belief in the Resurrection?

Jesus, you were shown to be the Son of God when you were raised from the dead by the power of the Holy Spirit. May I continue to believe that you are the Messiah, the Son of God, and that by believing in you I will have life by the power of your name.

ROMANS 1:4; JOHN 20:31

Our problems on earth hold us in bondage, tempting us to live in fear rather than in peace. However, having the assurance of eternity with God frees you from living in fear. Focus on this truth today. Talk to God about an impossible situation, person, or problem in your life. Remind yourself that if God can raise his Son from the dead, then surely he can do the impossible in your life.

BAPTISM IS A SYMBOL OF YOUR NEW LIFE IN CHRIST

Lord, what does baptism represent?
You were buried with Christ when you were baptized. And with him you were raised to new life because you trusted my mighty power that raised Christ from the dead.

COLOSSIANS 2:12

How different will my life be after baptism?
Since you have died to sin, how can you continue to live in it? Or have you forgotten that when you were joined with Christ Jesus in baptism, you joined him in his death? For you died and were buried with Christ by baptism. And just as Christ was raised from the dead by my glorious power, now you also may live a new life.

ROMANS 6:2-4

*What can I pray to stay committed to
this new life I've been given?*

Wash me clean from my guilt, O God. Purify me from
my sin. Purify me from my sins, and I will be clean;
wash me, and I will be whiter than snow.

PSALM 51:2, 7

*Baptism is an outward symbol of an inward change. Baptism is important
because it makes a public statement of your faith in Jesus. It is also important in
the life of the church, as each baptism celebrates the power of the gospel of Christ
to change lives. If you've been baptized, reflect on that moment. Has your life been
different since then? How so? If you haven't yet been baptized, prayerfully consider
whether you're ready for this next step of publicly confessing your faith.*

WHERE REAL SECURITY COMES FROM

Lord Jesus, how does knowing you help me feel secure?
Anyone who listens to my teaching and follows it is
wise, like a person who builds a house on solid rock.
I give you eternal life, and you will never perish. No
one can snatch you away from me. No one can snatch
you from the Father's hand.

MATTHEW 7:24; JOHN 10:28-29

How do I deal with my feelings of insecurity?
Since you have been made right in my sight by faith,
you have peace with me because of what Jesus Christ
your Lord has done for you. Because of your faith,
Christ has brought you into this place of undeserved
privilege where you now stand, and you may confidently and joyfully look forward to sharing my glory.
I am protecting you by my power until you receive
this salvation, which is ready to be revealed on the
last day for all to see.

ROMANS 5:1-2; I PETER I:5

*What can I pray when the world makes
me feel insecure and afraid?*

Nothing in all creation will ever be able to separate me
from your love, God. Because of your grace, you made
me right in your sight and gave me confidence that I
will inherit eternal life.

ROMANS 8:39; TITUS 3:7

*Governments shift and become unstable, relationships fall apart, and natural
disasters threaten our homes. We each have our own fears and worries. But
knowing God means we know the source of peace. You are tethered to God's
love, which keeps you connected to him until you safely reach your eternal
home. Tie a string around your wrist or finger this morning. When you feel
insecure, look at the string to remind yourself that God is your Savior and
your refuge, and nothing can snatch you from his hand.*

PUT YOUR ENERGY TOWARD THIS

Lord Jesus, what drains my energy and distracts me from what's really important?

Don't worry about everyday life—whether you have enough food and drink, or enough clothes to wear. Can all your worries add a single moment to your life? Spend your energy seeking the eternal life that I can give you. Don't look at the troubles you can see now; rather, fix your gaze on things that cannot be seen. For the things you see now will soon be gone, but the things you cannot see will last forever.

MATTHEW 6:25, 27; JOHN 6:27;
2 CORINTHIANS 4:18

What should I pour my energy into?

I am your God, the one and only. And you must love me with all your heart, all your soul, all your mind, and all your strength. And love your neighbor as yourself. No other commandment is greater than these.

MARK 12:29-31

How can I pray when I need to refocus my energy?
LORD, remind me how brief my time on earth will be.
Remind me that my days are numbered—how fleeting my life is. I focus on this one thing: Forgetting the past and looking forward to what lies ahead, I press on to reach the end of the race and receive the heavenly prize.

PSALM 39:4; PHILIPPIANS 3:13-14

We often spend our energy on what feels urgent, but how often do we spend our energy on things that matter for eternity? Look at your schedule for the week ahead. Where will the majority of your energy go? What distractions will keep you too busy to focus on loving God and others? As you look over the week ahead, ask God to help you focus on what's truly important from an eternal perspective.

SLOW DOWN AND SAVOR

Lord, why is it important to slow down sometimes?
Be still and know that I am God! I have made your
life no longer than the width of your hand. Your
entire lifetime is just a moment to me, and all your
busy rushing ends in nothing. How do you know
what your life will be like tomorrow? Your life is like
the morning fog—it's here a little while, then it's
gone. When Jesus said, "Let's go off by ourselves to
a quiet place and rest awhile," he said this because
there were so many people coming and going that
he and his apostles didn't even have time to eat.

PSALM 46:10; PSALM 39:5-6; JAMES 4:14;
MARK 6:31

What happens when I take time out of
my busy schedule to slow down?
Be still in my presence, and wait patiently for me to
act. Come to me, all of you who are weary and carry
heavy burdens, and I will give you rest. Take my yoke
upon you. Let me teach you, because I am humble
and gentle at heart, and you will find rest for your

souls. Only in returning to me and resting in me will you be saved. In quietness and confidence is your strength.

PSALM 37:7; MATTHEW 11:28-29; ISAIAH 30:15

What can I pray when I find myself always rushing? Those who live in the shelter of the Most High will find rest in the shadow of the Almighty. This I declare about you, LORD: You alone are my refuge, my place of safety; you are my God, and I trust you.

PSALM 91:1-2

When you rush through life, it's easy to miss out on all that God has waiting for you today. Intentionally fight against hurry by slowly reading the Bible verses on this page once again. Savor each word. Do you see anything you missed the first time you read through them?

GAINING CONFIDENCE STARTS HERE

Lord, how do I gain more confidence in myself, my faith, and my actions?

Trust in me with all your heart; do not depend on your own understanding. Blessed are those who trust in me and have made me their hope and confidence. They are like trees planted along the riverbank, bearing fruit each season. Their leaves never wither, and they prosper in all they do.

PROVERBS 3:5; JEREMIAH 17:7; PSALM 1:3

How can I live each day with a confident attitude?

Because of Christ and your faith in him, you can now come boldly and confidently into my presence. Seek my will in all you do, and I will show you which path to take.

EPHESIANS 3:12; PROVERBS 3:6

*What can I pray when troubling times
shake my confidence in you?*

You are my light and my salvation—so why should I
be afraid? Though a mighty army surrounds me, my
heart will not be afraid. Even if I am attacked, I will
remain confident. Teach me how to live, O LORD.
Lead me along the right path, for my enemies are
waiting for me. Yet I am confident I will see your
goodness.

PSALM 27:1, 3, 11, 13

*Do you see God as reliable? Do you feel you can count on him no matter
what? Confidence in God grows as you step out in faith and find that he is
there to catch you. Recount to yourself the times you've seen God come
through for you. Where has he rescued you, blessed you, protected you, and
provided for you? What is his track record in your life? How does this
give you confidence in the situations you're facing today?*

GOD LOOKS INSIDE

Lord, what makes a person truly beautiful?

Let your conversation be gracious and attractive so that you will have the right response for everyone. Do everything without complaining and arguing, so that no one can criticize you. Live clean, innocent lives as my children, shining like bright lights in a world full of crooked and perverse people. Don't be concerned about the outward beauty of fancy hairstyles, expensive jewelry, or beautiful clothes. You should clothe yourselves instead with the beauty that comes from within, the unfading beauty of a gentle and quiet spirit, which is so precious to me.

COLOSSIANS 4:6; PHILIPPIANS 2:14-15;
1 PETER 3:3-4

How can I learn to see beauty in others the way you see it?

Don't judge by appearance. I don't see things the way you see them. You judge by outward appearance, but I look at the heart.

1 SAMUEL 16:7

*What can I pray to better see the
inner beauty in others?*

Lord, when I look at the night sky and see the work
of your fingers—the moon and the stars you set in
place—what are mere mortals that you should think
about them, human beings that you should care for
them? Yet you made them only a little lower than
yourself and crowned them with glory and honor.

PSALM 8:3-5

*When you're with others, are you more focused on their inner or outer
appearance? Today, make a point to ask heart questions that can help illu-
minate the beauty within. Some examples might be, "What's the most
important thing going on in your life, and how do you feel about it?" or
"When are times you've felt the most happy/sad/scared?"*

WORDS THAT BRING HEALING

Lord, how can I best receive criticism?

Be quick to listen, slow to speak, and slow to get angry. Human anger does not produce the righteousness I desire. A fool is quick-tempered, but a wise person stays calm when insulted. If you listen to constructive criticism, you will be at home among the wise. Timely advice is lovely, like golden apples in a silver basket. To one who listens, valid criticism is like a gold earring or other gold jewelry.

JAMES 1:19-20; PROVERBS 12:16;
PROVERBS 15:31; PROVERBS 25:11-12

How can I give constructive advice?

Let us aim for harmony . . . and try to build each other up. Let everything you say be good and helpful, so that your words will be an encouragement to those who hear them. Some people make cutting remarks, but the words of the wise bring healing. Don't speak evil against others.

Encourage each other. Live in harmony and peace. Then my love and peace will be with you.

ROMANS 14:19; EPHESIANS 4:29; PROVERBS 12:18; JAMES 4:11; 2 CORINTHIANS 13:11

What can I pray when I am criticized or feel tempted to criticize others?

May the words of my mouth and the meditation of my heart be pleasing to you, O LORD, my rock and my redeemer.

PSALM 19:14

Criticism, constructive or not, is often hard to swallow. Constructive advice, though it may hurt, can bring about important growth. Have you ever received advice that hurt at the time but later facilitated change and growth in your life? How did you receive that advice? This morning, ask God for an openness to constructive advice from others and help to discern words of healing from voices of criticism. If you are in a relationship where you are constantly criticized and hurt verbally, please seek help. Abuse, even if it is verbal, is very different from helpful and timely advice.

EVEN IF OTHERS BETRAY YOU, GOD REMAINS FAITHFUL

Lord, why does betrayal hurt so much?

Telling lies about others is as harmful as hitting them with an ax, wounding them with a sword, or shooting them with a sharp arrow. As for [David's] companion, he betrayed his friends; he broke his promises. His words are as smooth as butter, but in his heart is war. His words are as soothing as lotion, but underneath are daggers!

PROVERBS 25:18; PSALM 55:20-22

Does your Word give me an example of how to handle relational brokenness?

Joseph replied, "Don't be afraid of me. Am I God, that I can punish you? You intended to harm me, but God intended it all for good. He brought me to this position so I could save the lives of many people. No, don't be afraid. I will continue to take care of you and your children." So he reassured them by speaking kindly to them.

GENESIS 50:19-21

*What can I pray to remind myself
of your faithfulness?*

Just because others are unfaithful, does that mean
you will be unfaithful, Lord? If I am unfaithful, you
remain faithful, for you cannot deny who you are.

ROMANS 3:3; 2 TIMOTHY 2:13

---

*Joseph was betrayed by his brothers and sold into slavery. But he trusted God
to redeem his hurt and pain and turn it into something good. Joseph chose to
forgive. When you forgive someone, writes Lewis Smedes, "you set a prisoner
free, but you discover that the real prisoner was [you]." Have you ever felt a
deep sense of betrayal? Ask God to help you forgive your betrayer so you can
be free from bitterness and resentment. Thank God that he is always faithful.*

GOD HAS GIVEN YOU A SPECIAL GIFT

Lord, do spiritual gifts still exist?
Do I have a spiritual gift?

I have given you a gift from my great variety of spiritual gifts. Use them well to serve others. To one person the Spirit gives the ability to give wise advice; to another the same Spirit gives a message of special knowledge. The same Spirit gives great faith to another, and to someone else the one Spirit gives the gift of healing.

I PETER 4:10; I CORINTHIANS 12:8-9

When I discover my spiritual gift,
how do I begin to use it?

If your gift is serving others, serve them well. If you are a teacher, teach well. If your gift is to encourage others, be encouraging. If it is giving, give generously. If I have given you leadership ability, take the responsibility seriously. And if you have a gift for showing kindness to others, do it gladly. If you need wisdom, ask me, and I will give it to you. Keep putting into practice all you learned. Make the most of every opportunity.

ROMANS 12:7-8; JAMES 1:5; PHILIPPIANS 4:9;
COLOSSIANS 4:5

What can I pray as I use my gifts to serve others?
O LORD, not to me, but to your name goes all the glory.

PSALM 115:1

God in his wisdom decided to use us to encourage and help people. The Holy Spirit has given every believer a spiritual gift for the purpose of helping others. Knowing your spiritual gift can help you decide where to participate in God's work. Do you know what your gift is? If not, take an online spiritual gifts assessment today (e.g., www.spiritualgiftstest.com). Ask close friends and family members what they think your spiritual gifts are and see how their answers line up with your assessment.

COMPASSION FOR CREATION

Lord, does it honor you if I'm a good steward of your creation?

I hold in my hands the depths of the earth and the mightiest mountains. The sea belongs to me, for I made it. My hands formed the dry land, too. Look! I have given you every seed-bearing plant throughout the earth and all the fruit trees for your food. I looked over all I had made, and I saw that it was very good!

PSALM 95:4-5; GENESIS 1:29, 31

What is my responsibility to care for the earth?

I, the LORD God, placed the man in the Garden of Eden to tend and watch over it. Then I blessed them and said, "Be fruitful and multiply. Fill the earth and govern it. Reign over the fish in the sea, the birds in the sky, and all the animals that scurry along the ground." The godly care for their animals, but the wicked are always cruel.

GENESIS 2:15; GENESIS 1:28; PROVERBS 12:10

What can I pray to remember that
this is your earth I take care of?

O LORD, what a variety of things you have made! In wisdom you have made them all. The earth is full of your creatures.

PSALM 104:24

Stewardship of the earth begins with the realization that everything on earth—plants, animals, and people—belongs to the Lord. If God took such care in creating the world, we should concern ourselves with nurturing and loving God's creation. Do something to make the earth more beautiful today. Start recycling, pick up litter, organize a seed and plant "share day" in your neighborhood, or donate to an organization that protects natural resources or promotes sustainable farming.

KEEP PRAYING EVEN WHEN GOD SEEMS SILENT

*Lord, what can I do when I feel
disconnected from you?*

Rejoice in your confident hope. Be patient in trouble,
and keep on praying. The earnest prayer of a righteous
person has great power and produces wonderful results.

ROMANS 12:12; JAMES 5:16

*Lord, I've prayed for something for a long time.
What if I never receive an answer?*

Why are you afraid? You have so little faith! It was by
faith that even Sarah was able to have a child, though
she was barren and was too old. She believed that I
would keep my promise. Keep on asking, and you
will receive what you ask for. Keep on seeking, and
you will find. Keep on knocking, and the door will
be opened to you. My grace is all you need. My
power works best in weakness.

MATTHEW 8:26; HEBREWS 11:11;
MATTHEW 7:7; 2 CORINTHIANS 12:9

*What can I pray when I am tempted
to give up praying?*

Lord, I am confident I will see your goodness. I will wait patiently for you. I will be brave and courageous. Yes, I will wait patiently for you, Lord.

PSALM 27:13-14

Steadfastness is a spiritual discipline that involves learning to endure patiently in your faith. Seasons of unanswered prayer can make you feel anything but steady or patient. Do you have prayers that still remain unanswered? Sometimes God chooses to answer prayers in unexpected ways. He promises to always answer them, though sometimes his answer is no.

Choose to remain steadfast in your prayers. Keep praying!

GOD'S WORD IS FULL OF LIVING POWER

The Bible was written so long ago. How can it be relevant to me today?

My word is alive and powerful. All my promises prove true. The grass withers, and the flowers fade, but my word stands forever. Study my commandments and reflect on my ways. Delight in my decrees and do not forget my word. My word is a lamp to guide your feet and a light for your path.

HEBREWS 4:12; PSALM 18:30; ISAIAH 40:8;
PSALM 119:15-16, 105

What is the power of Scripture? How does your Word guide me?

All Scripture is inspired by me and is useful to teach you what is true and to make you realize what is wrong in your life. It corrects you when you are wrong and teaches you to do what is right. I use it to prepare and equip my people to do every good work.

2 TIMOTHY 3:16-17

*What can I pray to open my heart to
be shaped by your Word?*

Your commandments give me understanding, Lord.
When I discovered your words, I devoured them.
They are my joy and my heart's delight. Oh, that my
actions would consistently reflect your decrees! Then
I will not be ashamed when I compare my life with
your commands. As I learn your righteous regulations,
I will thank you by living as I should!

PSALM 119:104; JEREMIAH 15:16;
PSALM 119:5-7

*Through reading and studying the Bible, you engage in a holy conversation
with God. His Word is a dynamic source of transformation and fruitfulness.
If God has the power to speak all of creation into existence, his written words
in Scripture have just as much transforming power. Reread the Scripture
passages above, reminding yourself of the active, living power that God's
Word holds. As you read, choose to trust that God is shaping your heart
to become more like his, even if you can't see it now.*

NO FAVORITES

Lord, do you favor some people more than others?

I created human beings in my own image. In my image I created them; male and female I created them. I show no favoritism. In every nation I accept those who fear me and do what is right. You are made right with me by placing your faith in Jesus Christ. And this is true for everyone who believes, no matter who they are.

GENESIS 1:27; ACTS 10:34-35; ROMANS 3:22

How should your lack of favoritism
affect the way I live?

Live in harmony with others. Don't be too proud to enjoy the company of ordinary people. And don't think you know it all! Always be humble and gentle. Be patient with others, making allowance for their faults because of your love. Make every effort to stay united in the Spirit, binding yourselves to others with peace.

ROMANS 12:16; EPHESIANS 4:2-3

*What can I pray when I find myself
playing favorites?*

Cleanse me from these hidden faults, O God. Keep me from deliberate sins! Don't let them control me. Make my love for all people grow and overflow. Help me do what is right, just, and fair.

PSALM 19:12-13; 1 THESSALONIANS 3:12;
PROVERBS 1:3

The world tries to rank people's worth based on their race, gender, ethnicity, political beliefs, and socioeconomic status. However, God's Word is counter-cultural and clear: He has no favorites. Every person is created in his image and has equal value. He loves every person he created. Therefore, we are to love all people equally as well. Are there some people whom you tend to favor over others? People who look like you? Those who are successful or more financially stable than others? Ask God to help your love for all people grow.

YOU ARE NEEDED IN GOD'S GREAT KINGDOM

Lord, what is the body of Christ?

Even before I made the world, I loved you and chose you in Christ to be holy and without fault in my eyes. I decided in advance to adopt you into my own family by bringing you to myself through Jesus Christ. This is what I wanted to do, and it gave me great pleasure. And the church is Christ's body; it is made full and complete by Christ, who fills all things everywhere with himself.

EPHESIANS 1:4-5, 23

How can I possibly make a difference in the body of Christ?

Just as your body has many parts and each part has a special function, so it is with Christ's body. There are many parts of Christ's body, and you all belong to each other. In my grace, I have given everyone different gifts for doing certain things well. I make the whole body fit together perfectly. As each part does its own special work, it helps the other parts grow, so that the whole body is healthy and growing and full of love.

ROMANS 12:4-6; EPHESIANS 4:16

What can I pray to motivate me to better serve the body of Christ?

I thank you, Christ Jesus my Lord, for you have given me strength to do your work. You considered me trustworthy and appointed me to serve you. Oh, how generous and gracious you are! You filled me with the faith and love that come from you, Christ Jesus.

I TIMOTHY 1:12, 14

The church is filled with people who have a wide variety of gifts and talents. Your role is to discover how God has gifted you and to use your gifts to serve others. Are you currently serving the body of Christ in some way? If not, consider where you might be useful and jump in. Ask your pastor what needs your church has. When you participate in the church, your faith is strengthened and God's Kingdom advances against the darkness.

WHEN SURRENDER BECOMES VICTORY

Lord, what does it mean to surrender my life to you?
I showed my great love for you by sending Christ to
die for you. Give yourself completely to me, for you
were dead, but now you have new life. If you try to
hang on to your life, you will lose it. But if you give
up your life for my sake, you will save it. For you died
to this life, and your real life is hidden with Christ in
me. And when Christ, who is your life, is revealed to
the whole world, you will share in all his glory.

ROMANS 5:8; ROMANS 6:13; MATTHEW 16:25;
COLOSSIANS 3:3-4

Does surrender always mean giving something up?
Is it worth it?
The Kingdom of Heaven is like a treasure that a
man discovered hidden in a field. In his excitement,
he hid it again and sold everything he owned to get
enough money to buy the field. Yes, everything else
is worthless when compared with the infinite value

of knowing Christ Jesus. Press on to reach the end of the race and receive the heavenly prize for which I, through Christ Jesus, am calling you.

MATTHEW 13:44; PHILIPPIANS 3:8, 14

What can I pray to surrender my life to you?
O LORD, you are my Father. I am the clay, and you are the potter. I am formed by your hand. O LORD, I give my life to you. I've given up everything to follow you. Give me understanding and I will obey your instructions; I will put them into practice with all my heart.

ISAIAH 64:8; PSALM 25:1; MARK 10:28;
PSALM 119:34

Surrendering to God means giving him control of your life. You can make plans, but always be open to God's plan for you. He always wants what is best for you. Read Philippians 3:8. What comes to mind as you think about the supreme value of knowing Christ? What areas in your life feel difficult to surrender to God?

INSPIRE THOSE AROUND YOU

Lord, how can I inspire others to know you?

You are the light of the world—like a city on a hilltop that cannot be hidden. No one lights a lamp and then puts it under a basket. Instead, a lamp is placed on a stand, where it gives light to everyone in the house. In the same way, let your good deeds shine out for all to see, so that everyone will praise me, your heavenly Father. And if someone asks about your hope as a believer, always be ready to explain it.

MATTHEW 5:14-16; 1 PETER 3:15

What actions might be most inspirational to others?

Keep on loving others as long as life lasts. Don't just pretend to love others. Really love them. Love each other with genuine affection, and take delight in honoring each other. Your love for one another will prove to the world that you are my disciples.

HEBREWS 6:11; ROMANS 12:9-10; JOHN 13:35

*What can I pray for those I hope
to inspire to follow you?*

Lord, may they have the power to understand, as all
your people should, how wide, how long, how high,
and how deep your love is. May they experience the
love of Christ, though it is too great to understand
fully. May they be made complete with all the fullness
of life and power that comes from you.

EPHESIANS 3:18-19

*If you want to inspire others to want to know God, learn how to love people well.
Live a life so overflowing with love that others can't help but notice—and wonder.
And when someone asks about your behavior, always be ready to explain your
faith with gentleness and respect. Whom in your sphere of influence might God
be calling you to love lavishly? How can you show him or her God's love today?*

YOUR GREATEST ADVOCATE

Lord Jesus, how does the Holy Spirit help me?
If you love me, obey my commandments. And I will
ask the Father, and he will give you another Advocate,
who will never leave you. He is the Holy Spirit, who
leads into all truth. When the Spirit of truth comes, he
will guide you into all truth. My Spirit gives you desires
that are opposite of what your sinful nature desires.

JOHN 14:15-17; JOHN 16:13; GALATIANS 5:17

How does the Holy Spirit advocate for me?
My Spirit, who raised Jesus from the dead, lives in
you. I will not abandon you as an orphan—I will
come to you. For my Spirit joins with your spirit to
affirm that you are my child. The Holy Spirit helps
you in your weakness. He prays for you with groanings that cannot be expressed in words. I know all
hearts and I know what the Spirit is saying, for the
Spirit pleads for you in harmony with my own will.

ROMANS 8:11; JOHN 14:18; ROMANS 8:16, 26-27

What can I pray in gratitude for the
Holy Spirit working on my behalf?

You are my strength and shield, Lord. I trust you
with all my heart. You help me, and my heart is filled
with joy. I burst out in songs of thanksgiving.

PSALM 28:7

The Holy Spirit affirms your identity as a child of God. The Holy Spirit
prays for you. And the Holy Spirit helps you desire the things that lead to
righteous living. How does it feel to know that the Holy Spirit is constantly
advocating for you? Is this comforting? Empowering? What does it mean to
you that you have a personal advocate in every season of your life?

GREAT EXPECTATIONS

Lord, what can I expect from you?

I am a faithful God who keeps my covenant for a thousand generations and lavishes my unfailing love on those who love me and obey my commands. I am merciful and compassionate, slow to get angry and filled with unfailing love. I am good to everyone. I shower compassion on all my creation. I always keep my promises; I am gracious in all I do.

DEUTERONOMY 7:9; PSALM 145:8-9, 13

How can I learn more about what
you have promised me?

Study my Book of Instruction continually. Meditate on it day and night. Let the message about Christ, in all its richness, fill your life. For all of my promises have been fulfilled in Christ with a resounding "Yes!" Hold tightly without wavering to the hope you affirm, for I can be trusted to keep my promise.

JOSHUA 1:8; COLOSSIANS 3:16; 2 CORINTHIANS 1:20;
HEBREWS 10:23

*How can I pray with expectation
of your faithfulness?*

I bow before your holy Temple as I worship. I praise your name for your unfailing love and faithfulness; for your promises are backed by all the honor of your name. As soon as I pray, you answer me; you encourage me by giving me strength.

PSALM 138:2-3

We can expect God to keep every promise he has given us in his Word. Allow God's promises to sink deep into your heart. The more you know God, the more his promises will provide you with strength, perseverance, and encouragement. Find a promise from God's Word and write it down. (Some suggestions: Psalm 32:8; Acts 16:31; 1 John 1:9; Isaiah 41:10; Romans 8:38.)

Meditate on this promise as you anticipate God's faithfulness to keep it.

LEARN TO DISCERN

Lord, why is discernment important?

My child, listen to what I say, and treasure my commands. Tune your ears to wisdom, and concentrate on understanding. Cry out for insight, and ask for understanding. Search for them as you would for silver; seek them like hidden treasures. Then you will understand what it means to fear the LORD, and you will gain knowledge of God. For the LORD grants wisdom! From his mouth come knowledge and understanding.

PROVERBS 2:1-6

What am I supposed to "discern"?

Listen to the words of the wise; apply your heart to my instruction. In this way, you may know the truth. For someone who lives on milk is still an infant and doesn't know how to do what is right. Solid food is for those who are mature, who through training have the skill to recognize the difference between right and wrong. Let those who are wise understand these things. Let those with discernment listen carefully.

My paths are true and right, and righteous people
live by walking in them.

PROVERBS 22:17, 21; HEBREWS 5:13-14;
HOSEA 14:9

What can I pray when I want greater understanding?
I pray that my love for others will overflow more and
more, and that I will keep on growing in knowledge
and understanding. For I want to understand what
really matters, so that I may live a pure and blameless
life until the day of Christ's return. Oh, that I might
know you, LORD! Let me press on to know you. You
will respond to me as surely as the arrival of dawn.

PHILIPPIANS 1:9-10; HOSEA 6:3

*Discernment is the process of training ourselves to recognize God's truth
and God's ways—to determine what pleases God and make decisions based on
wisdom and good judgment. It is necessary for growing in your faith. Before
each decision today—about what you say, what you eat, or how you spend
your time—ask whether your decision will lead you closer to God.*

CHANGE THIS FIRST

Lord, what most affects my actions?

It is what comes from inside that defiles you. For from within, out of a person's heart, come evil thoughts, sexual immorality, theft, murder, adultery, greed, wickedness, deceit, lustful desires, envy, slander, pride, and foolishness. But those who are controlled by the Holy Spirit think about things that please the Spirit. Letting your sinful nature control your mind leads to death. But letting the Spirit control your mind leads to life and peace.

MARK 7:20-22; ROMANS 8:5-6

How do I allow the Spirit to control my thoughts and actions?

Fix your thoughts on what is true, and honorable, and right, and pure, and lovely, and admirable. Think about things that are excellent and worthy of praise. Put on your new nature, and be renewed as you learn to know me, your Creator, and become like me.

PHILIPPIANS 4:8; COLOSSIANS 3:10

*What can I pray when I want to change
my thoughts and actions?*

Lord, thank you that I am not controlled by my sinful nature. I am controlled by your Spirit if I have him living in me.

ROMANS 8:9

Your thoughts guide your emotions and influence your actions. Allowing your mind to wander down paths of unhealthy and sinful thoughts will lead you far away from the kind of thoughts and attitudes that God desires. Choosing to dwell on things that honor God will help you focus better on loving him and others. This involves fixing your thoughts on him. What tends to prompt you to have sinful thoughts? Envy arising from social media? Lust from the movies you watch? Text Romans 8:9 to yourself to help you remember to ask the Spirit to guide your thoughts and actions.

FOLLOW GOD, NOT YOUR HEART

Lord, why can following my heart be dangerous?
The human heart is the most deceitful of all things, and desperately wicked. For from within, out of a person's heart, come evil thoughts, greed, wickedness, deceit, lustful desires, envy, slander, pride, and foolishness. When sin is allowed to grow, it gives birth to death. People begin to think up foolish ideas of what I am like. As a result, their minds become dark and confused. And instead of worshiping the glorious, ever-living God, they worship idols.

JEREMIAH 17:9; MARK 7:21-22; JAMES 1:15; ROMANS 1:21, 23

How do I follow you with all my heart?
My child, pay attention to what I say. Listen carefully to my words. Let them penetrate deep into your heart, for they bring life to those who find them. Just as you accepted Christ Jesus as your Lord, you must continue to follow him. Let your roots grow down into him,

and let your life be built on him. Then your faith will grow strong in the truth you were taught, and you will overflow with thankfulness.

PROVERBS 4:20-22; COLOSSIANS 2:6-7

How can I pray for a heart that longs to please you?
May you produce in me, through the power of Jesus Christ, every good thing that is pleasing to you.

HEBREWS 13:21

Following your heart can be dangerous if it means you make decisions based only on what you imagine is best—not on what God says is best for you. As sinful people, we are naturally tempted to choose paths that go against God's way for us. So how can you protect your heart and make wise decisions that please God? Fill your mind and heart with God's Word and ask him to give you the wisdom to live according to his truth. When making decisions, constantly ask, "Is this desire leading me toward or away from God and his Word?"

STEP INTO THE SADNESS OF ANOTHER

Lord, how can I help someone who is experiencing deep sadness?

Be happy with those who are happy, and weep with those who weep. Share each other's burdens. When three of Job's friends heard of the tragedy he had suffered, they got together and traveled from their homes to comfort and console him. Then they sat on the ground with him for seven days and nights. No one said a word to Job, for they saw that his suffering was too great for words.

ROMANS 12:15; GALATIANS 6:2; JOB 2:11, 13

How do you help me comfort others?

I am your merciful Father and the source of all comfort. I comfort you in all your troubles so that you can comfort others. When they are troubled, you will be able to give them the same comfort I have given you.

2 CORINTHIANS 1:3-4

What can I pray for someone who is experiencing deep sadness?

You hear your people when they call to you for help. You rescue them from all their troubles. You are close to the brokenhearted; you rescue those whose spirits are crushed. LORD, you know the hopes of the helpless. Surely you will hear their cries and comfort them.

PSALM 34:17-18; PSALM 10:17

Can you think of someone who is currently hurting? The Bible gives guidance on how to walk alongside others by offering your prayers, presence, help, and a listening ear. Don't allow the discomfort of seeing people sad make you try to explain or fix their pain. Simply choose to be with them and help them feel the love and presence of God through you. Who might God be calling you to reach out to or show comfort to in their sadness today? Ask him how he would like you to do this.

GO EMPTY TO BE
FILLED BY GOD

Lord, what Bible stories show us reasons to fast?
Jehoshaphat begged me for guidance. He also ordered everyone in Judah to begin fasting. So people from all the towns of Judah came to Jerusalem to seek my help. This is the kind of fasting I want: Free those who are wrongly imprisoned; lighten the burden of those who work for you. Let the oppressed go free, and remove the chains that bind people. Share your food with the hungry, and give shelter to the homeless. Give clothes to those who need them, and do not hide from relatives who need your help. The people of Nineveh believed my message, and from the greatest to the least, they declared a fast to show their sorrow.

2 CHRONICLES 20:3-4; ISAIAH 58:6-7; JONAH 3:5

How should I prepare to fast?
When you fast, don't make it obvious, as the hypocrites do, for they try to look miserable and disheveled so people will admire them for their fasting. That is the

only reward they will ever get. But when you fast, comb your hair and wash your face. Then no one will notice that you are fasting, except for me. I know what you do in private. I see everything, and I will reward you.

MATTHEW 6:16-18

What can I pray to prepare my heart for fasting?
I am counting on you, LORD; yes, I am counting on you. I have put my hope in your word. I long for you, Lord, more than sentries long for the dawn. I want to know you and experience the mighty power that raised Christ from the dead.

PSALM 130:5-6; PHILIPPIANS 3:10

Have you ever fasted as a spiritual exercise? Fasting is abstaining from food to gain a greater awareness of God's power and presence in your life. There is something about going without food that clears your mind to better focus on God. Ask the Lord if a fast is right for you. Start small by fasting for one or two meals. Use your hunger pangs as a reminder to pray.

STRENGTH BEYOND IMAGINATION

Lord, what is an example of how you use someone with weak faith to do something great?

Then I turned to Gideon and said, "Go with the strength you have, and rescue Israel from the Midianites. I am sending you!" "But Lord," Gideon replied, "how can I rescue Israel? My clan is the weakest in the whole tribe of Manasseh, and I am the least in my entire family!" I said to him, "I will be with you. And you will destroy the Midianites as if you were fighting against one man."

JUDGES 6:14-16

What can your power do through me?

In my strength you can crush an army; with me, you can scale any wall. I am the everlasting God, the Creator of all the earth. I never grow weak or weary. No one can measure the depths of my understanding. I give power to the weak and strength to the powerless.

2 SAMUEL 22:30; ISAIAH 40:28-29

What can I pray to help activate my faith in you?
I have been chosen to know you, believe in you,
and understand that you alone are God. There is no
other God—there never has been, and there never
will be. You, yes you, are the LORD, and there is no
other Savior. All glory to you, God, who is able,
through your mighty power at work within me,
to accomplish infinitely more than I might ask or
think.

ISAIAH 43:10-11; EPHESIANS 3:20

When you put your trust in God, you don't need to have the strongest faith in order for him to use you. Sometimes all you can offer is your weakest yes. Even then, fear can keep you from moving forward in confident faith. Do you feel like God is calling you to do something? What fears or concerns might be holding you back? How can faith in God help you move forward?

WHEN YOU WONDER WHAT YOU'RE SUPPOSED TO HOPE IN

Lord, what is the source of my hope?

Look up to the mountains—does your help come from there? Your help comes from me, who made heaven and earth! If your wealth increases, don't make it the center of your life. Power belongs to me; unfailing love is mine. I am the LORD, and I do not change. Put your hope in me. I am your help and your shield. In me your heart rejoices; trust in my holy name.

PSALM 121:1-2; PSALM 62:10-12;
MALACHI 3:6; PSALM 33:20-21

What happens if I start to place my hope in the wrong things?

Be sure that your faith is in me alone. Do not waver, for your divided loyalty makes you as unsettled as a wave of the sea that is blown and tossed by the wind. People like this should not expect to receive anything from me. Their loyalty is divided between me and the world, and they are unstable in everything they do. Give me your heart. May your eyes take delight in following my ways.

JAMES 1:6-8; PROVERBS 23:26

What can I pray to renew my hope that you alone will meet my greatest needs?
I trust in your unfailing love. I will rejoice because you have rescued me. I will sing to you, LORD, because you are good to me. Lead me by your truth and teach me, for you are the God who saves me. All day long I put my hope in you.

PSALM 13:5-6; PSALM 25:5

Examine where you turn for hope today. Is it to material things, financial stability, success, the love and acceptance of others, changed circumstances, having a comfortable life, healing? Ask yourself, Why do I turn to these things when I feel insecure? The world offers many things to help you live a better, healthier life, but never let these distract you from your ultimate hope in God's rescue plan. Pray Psalm 13:5-6 to proclaim that God alone is your rescuer and source of hope.

LET YOUR YES MEAN YES

*Lord, what can I learn from your Word about
the impact of telling lies?*

The tongue is a small thing that makes grand speeches.
But a tiny spark can set a great forest on fire. And
among all the parts of the body, the tongue is a flame
of fire. It is a whole world of wickedness, corrupting
your entire body. It can set your whole life on fire, for
it is set on fire by hell itself. Truthful words stand the
test of time, but lies are soon exposed. I detest lying
lips, but I delight in those who tell the truth.

JAMES 3:5-6; PROVERBS 12:19, 22

How can I learn to speak with genuine truthfulness?

Reject all shameful deeds and underhanded methods.
Don't try to trick anyone or distort my word. Tell the
truth before me. Never take an oath, by heaven or
earth or anything else. Just say a simple yes or no, so
that you will not sin and be condemned. Anything
beyond this is from the evil one.

2 CORINTHIANS 4:2; JAMES 5:12;
MATTHEW 5:37

What can I pray to confess lies and untruth?
I was born a sinner—yes, from the moment my
mother conceived me. But you desire honesty from
the womb, teaching me wisdom even there. Take
control of what I say, O LORD, and guard my lips.

PSALM 51:5-6; PSALM 141:3

*Think back over the past week. Did you ever say you would do
something—such as praying for a friend or setting a time to get together—
but not follow through? Were there any commitments you made but
bailed on at the last minute? Today, be intentional about letting your
yes mean yes. If there was anything this past week you didn't follow
through on, set aside time today to keep your commitment.*

LIVE AS A CITIZEN
OF HEAVEN

*Lord, why is it that following you sometimes makes
me feel as if I don't connect with my culture?*

You are only a foreigner in the land. You must live as a
citizen of heaven, conducting yourself in a manner worthy
of the Good News about Christ. Even when Abraham
reached the land I promised him, he lived there by faith—
for he was like a foreigner, living in tents. Abraham was
confidently looking forward to a city with eternal founda-
tions, a city designed and built by me.

PSALM 119:19; PHILIPPIANS 1:27; HEBREWS 11:9-10

What does it mean to live as a citizen of heaven?

Once you had no identity as a people; now you are
my people. I warn you as a "temporary resident and
foreigner" to keep away from worldly desires that
wage war against your very soul. I have told you what
is good, and this is what I require of you: to do what
is right, to love mercy, and to walk humbly with me,
your God. Set your sights on the realities of heaven,

where Christ sits in the place of honor at my right hand. Think about the things of heaven, not the things of earth. For you died to this life, and your real life is hidden with Christ in me.

1 PETER 2:10-11; MICAH 6:8; COLOSSIANS 3:1-3

What can I pray when I feel like an outsider?
Help me to live in reverent fear of you, God, during my time here as a "temporary resident." For I am not ashamed of this Good News about Christ. It is your power at work, saving everyone who believes.

1 PETER 1:17; ROMANS 1:16

The times when you long to connect to this world are meant to point to your deeper longing to connect to your heavenly home, where every need will be met by Christ. Reflect on the past week. When did things feel most right with the world? Where did the sense of rightness come from? Scripture? Culture? Try to evaluate each decision you make today from the perspective of being a "temporary resident" of this world.

A PERSPECTIVE TO BRING YOU THROUGH TOUGH TIMES

Lord, why do we suffer? Why don't you protect us from bad things?

Don't be surprised at the fiery trials you are going through, as if something strange were happening to you. Instead, be very glad—because these trials will make you partners with Christ in his suffering, so that you will have the wonderful joy of seeing his glory when it is revealed to all the world. I have told you all this so that you may have peace in me. Here on earth you will have many trials and sorrows. But take heart, because I have overcome the world.

I PETER 4:12-13; JOHN 16:33

What do you protect me from?

I am your hiding place; I protect you from trouble. I surround you with songs of victory. My faithful promises are your armor and protection. I order

my angels to protect you wherever you go. I am faithful; I will strengthen you and guard you from the
evil one.

PSALM 32:7; PSALM 91:4, 11;
2 THESSALONIANS 3:3

What can I pray when I don't feel safe or secure?
Even when I walk through the darkest valley, I will
not be afraid, for you are close beside me. Your rod
and your staff protect and comfort me.

PSALM 23:4

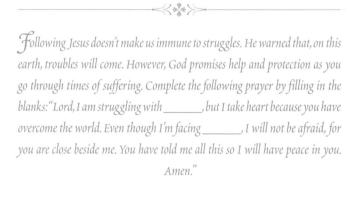

Following Jesus doesn't make us immune to struggles. He warned that, on this
earth, troubles will come. However, God promises help and protection as you
go through times of suffering. Complete the following prayer by filling in the
blanks: "Lord, I am struggling with _____, but I take heart because you have
overcome the world. Even though I'm facing _____, I will not be afraid, for
you are close beside me. You have told me all this so I will have peace in you.
Amen."

WHEN TRUST FACES UNCERTAINTY

Lord, how can I trust you when I'm dealing with great uncertainty?

I am the Alpha and the Omega—the beginning and the end. I am the one who is, who always was, and who is still to come—the Almighty One. I am the one who shaped the mountains, stirs up the winds, and reveals my thoughts to mankind. I turn the light of dawn into darkness and tread on the heights of the earth. The Lord God of Heaven's Armies is my name!

REVELATION 1:8; AMOS 4:13

What is something I can be certain of today?

Even in darkness you cannot hide from me. To me the night shines as bright as day. Darkness and light are the same to me. I saw you before you were born. Every day of your life was recorded in my book. Every moment was laid out before a single day had passed. You still belong to me; I hold your right hand. I guide you with my counsel, leading you to a glorious destiny.

PSALM 139:12, 16; PSALM 73:23-24

What can I pray when I'm anxious because of all the uncertainty in my life?
Let me hear of your unfailing love each morning, for I am trusting you. Show me where to walk, for I give myself to you. Teach me to do your will, for you are my God. May your gracious Spirit lead me forward on a firm footing.

PSALM 143:8, 10

Though you may be surprised and shaken by life's circumstances, God is not. Write down every quality that this morning's reading reveals about God's character. Make note of the ones you long to see more of. Prayerfully ask God to keep revealing these aspects of his character as you choose to trust him in life's uncertainty.

ENDING THE REBELLION

Lord, what happens when I rebel against you—
when I go ahead and do what I know I shouldn't?
Everyone who sins is breaking my law, for all sin is
contrary to my law. Anyone who keeps on sinning
does not know me or understand who I am. My eyes
watch over those who do right, and my ears are open
to their prayers. But I turn my face against those
who do evil.

   1 JOHN 3:4, 6; 1 PETER 3:12

Can you help me desire your life-giving ways?
Put all your rebellion behind you. I will give you a
new heart, and I will put a new spirit in you. I will
take out your stony, stubborn heart and give you a
tender, responsive heart. And I will put my Spirit in
you so that you will follow my decrees and be careful to obey my regulations. For I am working in
you, giving you the desire and the power to do what
pleases me.

   EZEKIEL 18:31; EZEKIEL 36:26-27;
   PHILIPPIANS 2:13

What truth can I pray to transform my rebellious heart?

For everyone has sinned; we all fall short of your glorious standard. Yet, in your grace, you freely make me right in your sight. You did this through Christ Jesus when he freed me from the penalty for my sins.

ROMANS 3:23-24

God's love is for everyone—rebel or righteous. Check your heart this morning. Would you describe it as soft and tender? Or is it hard and stony? Pray Ezekiel 36:26-27 over any known rebellion to the Lord and ask him to give you a tender and responsive heart to him in this area.

YOUR HEALTH
MAY FAIL YOU, BUT
GOD WILL NOT

Lord, how can I have hope in times of sickness?
Earthly bodies are planted in the ground when they
die, but they will be raised to live forever. Your body is
buried in brokenness, but it will be raised in glory. It
is buried in weakness, but it will be raised in strength.
I will wipe every tear from your eyes, and there will be
no more death or sorrow or crying or pain. All these
things will be gone forever.

1 CORINTHIANS 15:42-43; REVELATION 21:4

*What is a positive way I can respond in times
of personal sickness?*
Let all that you are praise me. Never forget the good
things I do for you. I forgive all your sins and heal all
your diseases. Your health may fail, and your spirit
may grow weak, but I remain the strength of your
heart; I am yours forever.

PSALM 103:2-3; PSALM 73:26

What can I pray to give me good perspective in my sickness?

Lord, three different times Paul begged you to take away the thorn in his flesh. Each time you said, "My grace is all you need. My power works best in weakness." So now I am glad to boast about my weaknesses, so that the power of Christ can work through me. When I am weak, then I am strong.

2 CORINTHIANS 12:8-10

Sickness can feel incredibly discouraging. When we experience physical pain, we can feel as if all of life is on hold. Though God hasn't promised us perfect health in this world, he promises it for his followers in the next world. Until then, meditate on this promise of health in heaven. This is a promise full of hope. Read 2 Corinthians 12:8-10 again. How can you use a physical ailment to remind yourself of God's presence and your need for him?

YOUR MOST IMPORTANT RELATIONSHIP

Lord, how do you invite me into relationship with you?

Your friendship with me was restored by the death of my Son while you were still my enemy. So now you can rejoice in your wonderful new relationship with me because Jesus Christ has made us friends. Your heart has heard me say, "Come and talk with me." And your heart responds, "LORD, I am coming."

ROMANS 5:10-11; PSALM 27:8

What do I talk about with you?

Give all your worries and cares to me, for I care about you. Don't worry about anything; instead, pray about everything. Tell me what you need, and thank me for all I have done. Then you will experience my peace, which exceeds anything you can understand. My peace will guard your heart and mind as you live in Christ Jesus.

1 PETER 5:7; PHILIPPIANS 4:6-7

What can I pray to respond to your invitation?
Speak, your servant is listening.

1 SAMUEL 3:10

God offers you a daily invitation to engage in relationship with him. Each day he invites you into his presence, wanting to both listen to you and share his counsel with you. There is no concern too small and no trouble too big. God invites you to pray, to tell him everything and exchange your worry for his peace. This morning, take out a sheet of paper and make three lists: one list of your needs, one list of your worries, and one list of things for which you are grateful to God. Pray through each item on the list in conversation with God. After each one, pause to listen and write down anything that comes to mind.

THE LORD WILL HELP YOU CARE FOR YOUR CHILDREN

*Lord, how do I raise children who grow
to know and love you?*

If you look for me wholeheartedly, you will find me.
Tell your children and grandchildren about the signs
I displayed—so you will know that I am the LORD.
Commit yourselves wholeheartedly to these words of
mine. Tie them to your hands and wear them on your
forehead as reminders. Teach them to your children.
Talk about them when you are at home and when you
are on the road, when you are going to bed and when
you are getting up. Direct your children onto the right
path, and when they are older, they will not leave it.

JEREMIAH 29:13; EXODUS 10:2;
DEUTERONOMY 11:18-19; PROVERBS 22:6

How will you help me with this huge task?

Do not be afraid or discouraged, for I will personally go ahead of you. I will be with you. I will feed

my flock like a shepherd. I will carry the lambs in my arms, holding them close to my heart. I will gently lead the mother sheep with their young.

DEUTERONOMY 31:8; ISAIAH 40:11

What can I pray over my children?
May the LORD bless you and protect you. May the LORD smile on you and be gracious to you. May the LORD show you his favor and give you his peace.

NUMBERS 6:24-26

Write down the prayer from Numbers 6. Place it somewhere you are often with your children—for example, above the changing table, on the dashboard of your car, or at the kitchen table—and use it to remind yourself to pray for them. Reread the prayer until you have it memorized.

HOW THOUGHTFUL ARE YOU?

Lord, how can I be more aware of the needs of those around me?
Don't be concerned for your own good but for the good of others. Don't be selfish; don't try to impress others. Be humble, thinking of others as better than yourself. Don't look out only for your own interests, but take an interest in others, too. Think of ways to motivate others to acts of love and good works.

I CORINTHIANS 10:24; PHILIPPIANS 2:3-4;
HEBREWS 10:24

How can I cultivate this selfless attitude toward others?
You know the generous grace of your Lord Jesus Christ. Though he was rich, yet for your sakes he became poor, so that by his poverty he could make you rich. For you have been called to live in freedom, my brothers and sisters. But don't use your freedom to satisfy your sinful nature. Instead, use your freedom to serve one another in love.

2 CORINTHIANS 8:9; GALATIANS 5:13

What can I pray when I'm feeling selfish?
May I always be full of joy in you, Lord. I say it
again—may I rejoice! Let everyone see that I am
considerate in all I do.

PHILIPPIANS 4:4-5

Reflect on the following questions and try to honestly assess how thought-
ful you are to those around you. Does it come naturally for you to do good to
others, or do you need to work at it? Do you forget birthdays, milestones, or
important events in the lives of people who are dear to you? Do you notice
when someone looks weary or burdened? Are you aware when someone
seems joyful or happy? Do you ask people about their lives, or do you do all
the talking? Ask God to open your eyes to see and open your heart to
respond to opportunities for practicing thoughtfulness today.

GOD NEVER CHANGES

Lord, can I really count on you to never change?
I am the LORD, and I do not change. My words will
never disappear. I am not a man, so I do not lie. I am
not human, so I do not change my mind. Have I ever
spoken and failed to act? Have I ever promised and
not carried it through? I can be trusted to keep my
promise.

MALACHI 3:6; MARK 13:31; NUMBERS 23:19;
HEBREWS 10:23

How should your constancy reassure my faith?
I am the faithful God who keeps my covenant for a
thousand generations and lavishes my unfailing love
on those who love me and obey my commands. You
have a priceless inheritance—an inheritance that is
kept in heaven for you, pure and undefiled, beyond
the reach of change and decay. I am your God forever
and ever, and I will guide you until you die.

DEUTERONOMY 7:9; I PETER 1:4; PSALM 48:14

What can I pray when change brings doubt?
I praise you, LORD, who have given rest to your people. Not one word has failed of all the wonderful promises you gave. The grass withers and the flowers fade, but your word stands forever.

1 KINGS 8:56; ISAIAH 40:8

Change is inevitable. Life keeps moving, and each season brings something new: a job change, a move, a promotion, a new baby, an empty nest, or an illness. But God has given his oath that he will never change. The strength of his unfailing love is as steady and sure today as it has always been. There is no transition you can pass through where God's love will cease to flow. Pick some flowers today or purchase them at the store. Enjoy their beauty, but as they fade and wither, remind yourself that God's promises will never fade but will endure forever.

YOU HAVE BEEN CHOSEN FOR GREAT THINGS

Lord, I feel so inadequate. How can you possibly use me to bring you glory?

I have not given you a spirit of fear and timidity, but of power, love, and self-discipline. Who dares accuse you, whom I have chosen for my own? No one—for I myself have given you right standing with me. Christ Jesus died for you and was raised to life for you, and he is sitting at my right hand, pleading for you. Overwhelming victory is yours through Christ, who loves you.

2 TIMOTHY 1:7; ROMANS 8:33-34, 37

Other people seem so confident. Am I the only one who struggles with feelings of inadequacy?

Moses pleaded with me, "O Lord, I'm not very good with words. I never have been, and I'm not now, even though you have spoken to me. I get tongue-tied, and my words get tangled." Then I asked Moses, "Who makes a person's mouth? Is it not I, the LORD? Now go! I will be with you as you speak, and I will instruct you in what to say." My grace is all you need. My power works best in weakness.

EXODUS 4:10-13; 2 CORINTHIANS 12:9

*What can I pray to battle against
my feelings of inadequacy?*
Lord, help me to remember that I can do everything through Christ, who gives me strength.

PHILIPPIANS 4:13

Moses demonstrates that overwhelming victory is possible when the God of the universe loves you and is for you! Moses also dealt with feelings of inadequacy, but God loves to use imperfect people to carry out his perfect plans. Why? Because his power shines brightest when he uses us despite our weaknesses. To battle feelings of inadequacy today, ask yourself, "Who made my _____ (body, personality, whatever you're struggling with)?" Hear God's words to Moses: "Now go! I will be with you and instruct you!"

AVOIDING THE MONEY TRAP

Lord, how can I keep a balanced mind-set about money?

Don't love money; be satisfied with what you have. For I have said, "I will never fail you. I will never abandon you." People who long to be rich fall into temptation and are trapped by many foolish and harmful desires that plunge them into ruin and destruction.

HEBREWS 13:5; I TIMOTHY 6:9

How can I keep from worrying about money all the time?

Everything you have comes from me, and you can give only what I first gave you! It is more blessed to give than to receive.

I CHRONICLES 29:14; ACTS 20:35

What can I pray to guide my
perspective about money?

Lord, your Word says that light shines in the darkness
for the godly. They are generous, compassionate, and
righteous. Good comes to those who lend money generously and conduct their business fairly. Such people
will not be overcome by evil. Those who are righteous
will be long remembered.

PSALM 112:4-6

Though our need for money is real, God makes it clear that the love of money is
destructive. When we elevate money above God, it throws our perspective out of
balance. Take an inventory of last month's expenses. Do your finances reflect gen-
erosity? Selfishness? Lack of faith? What nonessential item did you spend the most
on last month? What might this reveal about your current perspective on money?

MAKING YOUR TIME COUNT

Lord, what does the Bible teach about laziness?

Despite their desires, the lazy will come to ruin, for their hands refuse to work. I walked by the field of a lazy person, the vineyard of one with no common sense. I saw that it was overgrown with nettles. It was covered with weeds, and its walls were broken down. A little extra sleep, a little more slumber, a little folding of the hands to rest—then poverty will pounce on you like a bandit; scarcity will attack you like an armed robber.

PROVERBS 21:25; PROVERBS 24:30-31, 33-34

What mind-set can help me be more productive?

A hard worker has plenty of food, but a person who chases fantasies has no sense. Lazy people want much but get little, but those who work hard will prosper. Never be lazy, but work hard and serve me enthusiastically. Work willingly at whatever you do, as though you were working for me rather than for people.

PROVERBS 12:11; PROVERBS 13:4;
ROMANS 12:11; COLOSSIANS 3:23

What can I pray when I feel like wasting time?
Lord, help me to never get tired of doing good.

2 THESSALONIANS 3:13

There is a difference between laziness and rest. Rest is a reward for hard work, but laziness produces nothing. It is closely tied to selfishness because lazy people expect others to do the work. Take a time assessment today. Keep a log of work time versus idle time. How much time do you spend scanning your phone or social media? How much TV do you watch? How much time is spent being productive (including productive rest)? How much time do you waste? Ask the Lord to reveal where there is laziness in your life and how you might use that time more fruitfully.

HOW TO MEASURE YOUR GROWTH

Lord, how can I know whether I am growing toward spiritual maturity?

Those who remain in me, and I in them, will produce much fruit. When you produce much fruit, you are my true disciples. The Holy Spirit produces this kind of fruit in your life: love, joy, peace, patience, kindness, goodness, faithfulness, gentleness, and self-control. Let your roots grow down into me, and let your life be built on me. Then your faith will grow strong in the truth you were taught.

JOHN 15:5, 8; GALATIANS 5:22-23; COLOSSIANS 2:7

What are a few practical ways to start maturing in my faith?

Remain faithful to the things you have been taught. Let the message about Christ, in all its richness, fill your life. Teach and counsel others with all the wisdom Christ gives.

2 TIMOTHY 3:14; COLOSSIANS 3:16

*What can I pray when I feel discouraged
about my growth?*

I am certain that you, God, who began the good work within me, will continue your work until it is finally finished on the day when Christ Jesus returns. I pray that I will keep on growing in knowledge and understanding. For I want to live a pure and blameless life until the day of Christ's return. May I always be filled with the fruit of my salvation—the righteous character produced in my life by Jesus Christ—for this will bring you much glory and praise, Lord. Grant me the joy of your presence and the pleasures of living with you forever.

PHILIPPIANS 1:6, 9-11; PSALM 16:11

Spiritual growth can feel like two steps forward and one step back. But remember: even incremental progress means you're growing. Don't be discouraged when your growth feels slow or at a plateau. God will continue his good work in you as you pursue him.

PRAYER REALLY
DOES MATTER

Lord, does it really matter if I pray for others?
The earnest prayer of a righteous person has great
power and produces wonderful results. Pray for all
people. Ask me to help them; intercede on their
behalf, and give thanks for them.

JAMES 5:16; 1 TIMOTHY 2:1

*What Bible stories show that prayer
makes a difference?*
Abraham approached me and said, "Will you sweep
away both the righteous and the wicked? Suppose
you find fifty righteous people living there in the
city—will you not spare it for their sakes?" I replied,
"If I find fifty righteous people in Sodom, I will spare
the entire city for their sake." Finally, Abraham said,
"Lord, please don't be angry with me. Suppose only
ten are found there?" And I replied, "Then I will not
destroy it for the sake of the ten."

GENESIS 18:23-24, 26, 32

What can I pray when I'm interceding for someone?
Father, the Creator of everything in heaven and on earth, I pray that from your glorious, unlimited resources you will empower me with inner strength through your Spirit. May I have the power to understand how wide, how long, how high, and how deep your love is. May I experience the love of Christ, though it is too great to understand fully. Then I will be made complete with all the fullness of life and power that comes from you.

EPHESIANS 3:14-16, 18-19

Intercession means talking to God on behalf of someone else. We are called to pray earnestly for others, trusting God to produce wonderful results from our faithful prayers. Don't be discouraged if you think your prayers are ineffective or unimportant. Ask God to give you faith and humility as you pray for others.

CARE FOR YOUR BODY BECAUSE IT IS A GIFT FROM GOD

Lord, what makes my body special?

Don't you realize that your body is the temple of the Holy Spirit, who lives in you and was given to you by me? You do not belong to yourself, for I bought you with a high price. So you must honor me with your body.

1 CORINTHIANS 6:19-20

If my body belongs to you, do I have a say in what I get to do?

You say, "I am allowed to do anything"—but not everything is good for you. Your body was made for me, and I care about your body. Do not let any part of your body become an instrument of evil to serve sin. Instead, give yourself completely to me, for you were dead, but now you have new life. So use your whole body as an instrument to do what is right for my glory.

1 CORINTHIANS 6:12-13; ROMANS 6:13

How can I pray about my body?

You made all the delicate, inner parts of my body and knit me together in my mother's womb. Thank you for making me so wonderfully complex! Your workmanship is marvelous—how well I know it.

PSALM 139:13-14

Your body is a gift from God. When you don't respect or care for your body, you break down the very vessel God wants to use to help accomplish his work in the world. If you think about your body as being the temple of the Holy Spirit, what are some ways you can care for and respect it? Exercise more? Drink more water? Get more rest? Eat healthier food? Choose one area to focus on this week.

HOW TO LOVE THOSE WITH WHOM YOU DISAGREE

Lord, how can I handle disagreements in a way that is pleasing to you?

Do all that you can to live in peace with everyone. A servant of mine must not quarrel but must be kind to everyone and be patient with difficult people. Clothe yourself with tenderhearted mercy, kindness, humility, gentleness, and patience. Make allowance for others' faults, and forgive anyone who offends you. Remember, I forgave you, so you must forgive others. Above all, clothe yourself with love, which binds everyone together in perfect harmony.

ROMANS 12:18; 2 TIMOTHY 2:24;
COLOSSIANS 3:12-14

But sometimes I get so angry. How can I keep quarrels from spiraling out of control?

Don't retaliate with insults when people insult you. Instead, pay them back with a blessing. That is what

I have called you to do, and I will bless you for it. A gentle answer deflects anger, but harsh words make tempers flare. Don't sin by letting anger control you. Think about it overnight and remain silent.

1 PETER 3:9; PROVERBS 15:1; PSALM 4:4

How can I pray for my difficult relationships?
May you, Lord, the one who gives patience and encouragement, help me live in complete harmony with others, as is fitting for followers of Christ Jesus.

ROMANS 15:5

We are imperfect people, navigating imperfect relationships. Sometimes, disagreements lead to greater understanding, intimacy, and depth of relationship. Other times they result in angry words, bitterness, and brokenness. How we choose to resolve an argument is extremely important. Think of a challenging relationship in your life right now. Read the Scriptures above and write down the adjectives that describe a person who works for peace. Which specific adjectives can you practice in this challenging relationship today?

DON'T LET BUSYNESS DISCONNECT YOU FROM GOD

*Lord, how can I cultivate a deeper relationship
with you when life is so busy?*
Jesus often withdrew to the wilderness for prayer.
Listen carefully to what I am saying, for I speak peace
to my faithful people. Do not return to your foolish
ways. Wait quietly before me, for your hope is in me.
Come close to me, and I will come close to you.

LUKE 5:16; PSALM 85:8; PSALM 62:5; JAMES 4:8

What happens when I make space for you?
I give you more and more grace and peace as you grow
in your knowledge of me. By my divine power, I have
given you everything you need for living a godly life.
You have received all of this by coming to know me,
the one who called you to myself by means of my marvelous glory and excellence.

2 PETER 1:2-3

*What can I pray when I need to withdraw
to connect with you?*

I wait quietly before you, God, for my victory comes
from you. My heart has heard you say, "Come and
talk with me." And my heart responds, "Lord, I am
coming."

PSALM 62:1; PSALM 27:8

*Despite the busyness of his ministry, Jesus often withdrew to connect with
his Father. When you make space for God, he increases your capacity for
grace and peace. You can receive so much from him, but only when you go to
him to be filled. Look at your schedule for this week. Is there any time to
connect with God? If not, what can you give up to make space for him? Try
to find a regular time in your schedule to listen to and connect with God.*

GOD'S FAITHFULNESS WILL CHANGE YOU

Lord, how can I see your faithfulness to me?
Never forget the good things I do for you. I forgive
all your sins and heal all your diseases. I redeem you
from death and crown you with love and tender
mercies. I fill your life with good things. Your youth
is renewed like the eagle's! My love remains forever
with those who fear me. My salvation extends to the
children's children of those who are faithful to my
covenant, of those who obey my commandments!

PSALM 103:2-5, 17-18

How can you be so consistently faithful,
even when I'm not faithful to you?
Can a mother forget her nursing child? Can she feel no
love for the child she has borne? Even if that were possible, I would not forget you! See, I have written your
name on the palms of my hands. If you are unfaithful,
I remain faithful, for I cannot deny who I am.

ISAIAH 49:15-16; 2 TIMOTHY 2:13

What can I pray to remind myself
of your faithfulness?

I will proclaim the name of the LORD; how glorious is our God! LORD, you are the Rock; your deeds are perfect. Everything you do is just and fair. You are a faithful God who does no wrong; how just and upright you are!

DEUTERONOMY 32:3-4

Faithfulness is part of God's essential character—he cannot forget those he made and loves. Meditate on how you've personally seen God's faithfulness. Think about a time when God answered your prayers. What were you praying about? What was his answer? Whether his answer was yes or no, how was it an example of God's faithfulness to you?

MORNING

47

GOD DELIGHTS IN YOU

Lord, in what do you delight?
I delight in those with integrity. I detest evil plans,
but I delight in pure words. I delight in those who tell
the truth. I delight in the prayers of the upright. I will
delight in you if you obey my voice and keep my
commands and decrees, and if you turn to me with
all your heart and soul.

PROVERBS 11:20; PROVERBS 15:26; PROVERBS 12:22;
PROVERBS 15:8; DEUTERONOMY 30:10

How do you express your delight in me?
How can I recognize it?
I delight in my people; I crown the humble with victory. I direct the steps of the godly. I delight in every
detail of their lives. Though they stumble, they will
never fall, for I hold them by the hand. I correct those
I love, just as a father corrects a child in whom he
delights. I led you to a place of safety; I rescued you
because I delight in you.

PSALM 149:4; PSALM 37:23-24; PROVERBS 3:12;
2 SAMUEL 22:20

*What can I pray to express my
delight in you, Lord?*

May all who search for you be filled with joy and
gladness in you. May those who love your salvation repeatedly shout, "The LORD is great!" Give
me happiness, O Lord, for I give myself to you.

PSALM 40:16; PSALM 86:4

*In any relationship, thoughtfulness toward each other promotes feelings of joy
and delight. How often do you ask God what delights him? How often do you
ask yourself what would bring joy to his heart? Try to go through your day
with this mind-set. How might this affect your attitude and choices today?*

CLING TO THIS ADVICE

Lord, what is your most important piece of advice?
You must love me, the LORD your God, with all your
heart, all your soul, and all your mind. This is the
first and greatest commandment. A second is equally
important: Love your neighbor as yourself.

MATTHEW 22:37-39

What does real love look like?
Love is patient and kind. Love is not jealous or boastful
or proud or rude. It does not demand its own way. It is
not irritable, and it keeps no record of being wronged.
It does not rejoice about injustice but rejoices whenever
the truth wins out. Love never gives up, never loses faith,
is always hopeful, and endures through every circumstance. Keep on loving others as long as life lasts.

I CORINTHIANS 13:4-7; HEBREWS 6:11

What can I pray to follow your advice to love others?
Lord, help me to remember that if I could speak all
the languages of earth and of angels, but didn't love

100

others, I would only be a noisy gong or a clanging cymbal. If I had such faith that I could move mountains, but didn't love others, I would be nothing. If I gave everything I have to the poor and even sacrificed my body, I could boast about it; but if I didn't love others, I would have gained nothing. Three things will last forever—faith, hope, and love—and the greatest of these is love.

I CORINTHIANS 13:1-3, 13

God's best piece of advice is to love him with all your heart, soul, and mind and to love others as yourself. Think of one person God might be calling you to love today. How can you love him or her the way Scripture encourages you to?

PAYING ATTENTION
TO RED FLAGS

*Lord, how can I tell if I'm wanting something
that's not good for me?*

You want what you don't have, so you scheme and
kill to get it. You are jealous of what others have, and
you can't possess it, so you fight and wage war to
take it away from them. Yet you don't have what you
want because you don't ask me for it. And even when
you ask, you don't get it because your motives are all
wrong—you want only what will give you pleasure.

JAMES 4:2-3

*Can you help me pursue what you know
is best for me?*

Let the Spirit renew your thoughts and attitudes. Put
on your new nature, created to be like mine—truly
righteous and holy. The sinful nature wants to do evil,
which is just the opposite of what the Spirit wants. And
the Spirit gives you desires that are the opposite of what
the sinful nature desires. I will give you a new heart, and

I will put a new spirit in you. I will take out your stony, stubborn heart and give you a tender, responsive heart. And I will put my Spirit in you so that you will follow my decrees and be careful to obey my regulations.

EPHESIANS 4:23-24; GALATIANS 5:17; EZEKIEL 36:26-27

What can I pray to keep my desires in line with yours?
Lord, with all my heart I want your blessings. Be merciful as you promised. Whom have I in heaven but you? I desire you more than anything on earth.

PSALM 119:58; PSALM 73:25

God created us with the capacity to desire. These desires can be powerful, motivating, and exciting. But they can also distract us and even destroy our lives. What are you desiring right now? Do you find yourself scheming to make it happen, feeling jealous or anxious? Pray the prayer above and ask God to raise red flags about any misplaced desires. Ask him to replace those desires with ones that are pleasing to him.

AN INTIMATE GIFT

Lord, why did you create sex?

I created human beings in my own image; male and female I created them. I blessed them and said, "Be fruitful and multiply. Fill the earth and govern it." This explains why a man leaves his father and mother and is joined to his wife, and the two are united into one. This is a great mystery, but it is an illustration of the way Christ and the church are one.

GENESIS 1:27-28; GENESIS 2:24; EPHESIANS 5:32

Why did you establish such specific guidelines for sex?

You can't say that your body was made for sexual immorality. It was made for me, and I care about your body. Give honor to marriage, and remain faithful to one another in marriage. Don't you realize that your body is the temple of the Holy Spirit, who lives in you and was given to you by me? My will is for you to be holy, so stay away from all sexual sin. Live in holiness and honor—not in lustful passion.

1 CORINTHIANS 6:13; HEBREWS 13:4;

1 CORINTHIANS 6:19; 1 THESSALONIANS 4:3-5

What can I pray if my sexual history is painful?
LORD, you say, "Come now, let's settle this." Though
my sins are like scarlet, you will make them as white
as snow.

ISAIAH 1:18

God created sex to be the ultimate act of intimacy between a man and a woman, uniting both body and soul in the covenant of marriage. Sex outside of marriage mistreats the body, damages the soul, and hinders our capacity for true intimacy. God's view of sexuality is far more fulfilling than the world's. He wants sex to bring joy and blessing within a marriage relationship. Whatever your sexual history, God is able to heal, restore, and redeem you and your relationships. Read the verses above again slowly, and talk to God about what stands out to you. He can wipe away any shame, guilt, or regret you feel and make you clean and pure again in his eyes.

TUNE IN TO WISDOM

Lord, how can I know what you want from me?
Be still, and know that I am God! My child, listen to
what I say, and treasure my commands. Tune your
ears to wisdom, and concentrate on understanding.
Cry out for insight, and ask for understanding. Search
for them as you would for silver; seek them like hidden treasures. Then you will understand what it means
to fear me, and you will gain knowledge of me. For I
grant wisdom! From my mouth come knowledge and
understanding.

PSALM 46:10; PROVERBS 2:1-6

How does wisdom foster a more discerning heart?
A wise person is hungry for knowledge, while the fool
feeds on trash. Wise people treasure knowledge, but the
babbling of a fool invites disaster. Wisdom is enshrined
in an understanding heart. For wisdom will enter your
heart, and knowledge will fill you with joy. Wise choices
will watch over you. Understanding will keep you safe.

PROVERBS 15:14; PROVERBS 10:14;
PROVERBS 14:33; PROVERBS 2:10-11

What can I pray to gain more wisdom from you?
O God, you are my God; I earnestly search for you.
My soul thirsts for you. Fear of you is the foundation
of true wisdom. All who obey your commandments
will grow in wisdom. Give me an understanding heart
so that I can know the difference between right and
wrong.

PSALM 63:1; PSALM 111:10; I KINGS 3:9

*A discerning heart hungers and thirsts for God, the source of wisdom
and knowledge. Today, practice tuning your ears to wisdom. Read a
psalm aloud (Psalms 27, 34, 51, and 103 are good choices). Pay careful attention to the words and how they affect you. What message are you receiving?
What did you learn about wise living?*

FAITH DOESN'T HAVE TO BE COMPLICATED

Lord, what does it mean to have faith?
Faith shows the reality of what you hope for; it is the evidence of things you cannot see. By faith you understand that the entire universe was formed at my command, that what you now see did not come from anything that can be seen. And it is impossible to please me without faith. If you want to come to me, you must believe that I exist and that I reward those who sincerely seek me.

HEBREWS 11:1, 3, 6

Is it really as simple as choosing to believe in you?
Don't be afraid. Just have faith. For my Kingdom belongs to those who are like children. I tell you the truth, anyone who doesn't receive my Kingdom like a child will never enter it.

MARK 5:36; LUKE 18:16-17

*What can I pray to encourage my
heart to simply trust?*

I called on your name, LORD: "Please, LORD, save me!" How kind you are! How good you are! So merciful, O God of mine! You protect those of childlike faith; I was facing death, and you saved me. Let my soul be at rest again, for you have been good to me.

PSALM 116:4-7

Faith is simply choosing to trust what you cannot always see—in this case, that God exists and that he is loving and good. If you have not taken this step of faith, it's not too late. Even now, God whispers, "Don't be afraid. Just have faith." He is waiting to show you his goodness and mercy. Do you believe? Pray the prayer above as a confession of your choice to simply trust God.

HOPE FOR HEALING

*What is an example from Scripture of your
healing and redeeming of past hurts?*

I redeemed Israel from those too strong for them.
They will be radiant because of my good gifts—
the abundant crops of grain, new wine, and olive
oil, and the healthy flocks and herds. Their life
will be like a watered garden, and all their sorrows
will be gone. I will turn their mourning into joy.
I will comfort them and exchange their sorrow
for rejoicing.

JEREMIAH 31:11-13

*What are some ways you might bring
healing in my life?*

Never forget my commandments, for by them I give
you life. My discipline is good, for it leads to life and
health. I restore your health and allow you to live!
I will restore to you the joy of your salvation, and
make you willing to obey me.

PSALM 119:93; ISAIAH 38:16; PSALM 51:12

What can I pray as I hope for healing?
Create in me a clean heart, O God. Renew a loyal
spirit within me. Renew my life with your goodness.
You have allowed me to suffer much hardship, but
you will restore me to life again and lift me up from
the depths of the earth.

PSALM 51:10; PSALM 119:40; PSALM 71:20

The best place to begin a journey of healing is by inviting Jesus into your pain. Often a physical act, such as kneeling, precedes a heart response. Get down on your knees before God (or lie on a bed if you can't kneel) as a symbol of your readiness to talk to him about your pain, and ask him to begin the process of healing your heart. Prayerfully consider the next step in your healing, such as seeing a counselor, memorizing Scripture, giving or receiving forgiveness, or pursuing reconciliation.

A HEART IN TUNE
WITH HIS

*Lord, how can my heart be more
aligned with yours?*

Keep away from anything that might take my place in
your heart. Don't ask for only what will give you pleasure. Don't you realize that friendship with the world
makes you my enemy? If you want to be a friend of
the world, you make yourself my enemy. Jesus prayed,
"I want your will to be done, not mine." Submit yourself to me. I will teach you my ways, that you may live
according to my truth! I will grant you purity of heart,
that you may honor me.

I JOHN 5:21; JAMES 4:3-4; MATTHEW 26:39;
2 CHRONICLES 30:8; PSALM 86:11

*What will I experience when my heart
is in tune with yours?*

You can be confident that I hear you whenever you
ask for anything that pleases me. I am close to all who
call on me, yes, to all who call on me in truth. I grant
the desires of those who fear me; I hear their cries for

help and rescue them. Take delight in me, and I will give you your heart's desires.

1 JOHN 5:14; PSALM 145:18-19; PSALM 37:4

How can I pray in line with your desires?
Father in heaven, may your name be kept holy. May your Kingdom come soon. May your will be done on earth, as it is in heaven. O LORD, do good to those whose hearts are in tune with you.

MATTHEW 6:9-10; PSALM 125:4

Are you in the middle of making a decision or dealing with a difficult circumstance that is out of your control? How might it change your attitude to pray, "Lord, I want your will to be done, not mine"? Let this be your prayer so that your desires will stay in tune with God's desires for you.

GOD GRIEVES WHEN HIS LOVED ONES DIE

Whose example can I follow to bear the grief of losing someone I love, Jesus? Are you with me in my sadness?

When I arrived at Bethany, I was told that Lazarus had already been in his grave for four days. When I saw Mary weeping and saw the other people wailing with her, I was deeply troubled. "Where have you put him?" I asked them. They told me, "Lord, come and see." Then I wept. I care deeply when my loved ones die.

JOHN 11:17, 33-35; PSALM 116:15

How do I cope, Lord Jesus? What hope is there in my grief?

Then I shouted, "Lazarus, come out!" And the dead man came out, his hands and feet bound in grave-clothes, his face wrapped in a headcloth. I told them, "Unwrap him and let him go!" I am the resurrection and the life. Anyone who believes in me will live, even after dying. Everyone who lives in me and believes in me will never ever die. Do you believe this?

JOHN 11:43-44; JOHN 11:25-26

What can I pray to find hope in the face of death?
You will remove the cloud of gloom, the shadow of death that hangs over the earth. You will swallow up death forever! Sovereign LORD, you will wipe away all tears.

ISAIAH 25:7-8

Jesus had many emotions about the death of his friend, which means it's okay for you to grieve your loss too. Your pain, tears, and emotions do not overwhelm or burden God. In fact, he welcomes them. Expressing your grief to God and others is part of healing. Read the prayer above again, asking God to help you have hope in eternity as you grieve your loss on earth.

THE END OF THE STORY

Lord, what are your plans for the future?
I am creating new heavens and a new earth, and no one will even think about the old ones anymore. Look, my home will now be among my people! I will live with them, and they will be my people. I will wipe every tear from their eyes, and there will be no more death or sorrow or crying or pain. All these things will be gone forever.

ISAIAH 65:17; REVELATION 21:3-4

How does this give me hope for my future?
That is why you never give up. Though your body is dying, your spirit is being renewed every day. For your present troubles are small and won't last very long. Yet they produce for you a glory that vastly outweighs them and will last forever! So don't look at the troubles you can see now; rather, fix your gaze on things that cannot be seen. For the things you see now will soon be gone, but the things you cannot see will last forever.

2 CORINTHIANS 4:16-18

What can I pray to maintain an eternal perspective?
Lord, help me to live as a citizen of heaven, conducting myself in a manner worthy of the Good News about Christ.

PHILIPPIANS 1:27

Your greatest hope is knowing the story of your future. For those who love God, that future includes the eternal joy and glories of a new earth—a place so wonderful it will far outweigh even the greatest happiness you have experienced on this earth. Pause and reflect on your story. What are you struggling with in this current season? What have you had to suffer in the past? Say a word of praise to God that he is the author of your story. Even though you have trials and conflicts, your ending will be complete healing and renewal for all eternity.

ADVERSITY IS NEVER WASTED

Lord, can anything good come from my troubles and difficulties?

I am your merciful Father and the source of all comfort. I comfort you in all your troubles so that you can comfort others. When others are troubled, you will be able to give them the same comfort I have given you. When troubles of any kind come your way, consider it an opportunity for great joy. For you know that when your faith is tested, your endurance has a chance to grow. Endurance develops strength of character, and character strengthens your confident hope of salvation. And this hope will not lead to disappointment.

2 CORINTHIANS 1:3-4; JAMES 1:2-3; ROMANS 5:4-5

What if I can't handle the trials ahead? Will you help me?

I am your refuge and strength, always ready to help in times of trouble. Don't be afraid, for I am with you. Don't be discouraged, for I am your God. I will strengthen you and help you. I will hold you up with my victorious right hand.

PSALM 46:1; ISAIAH 41:10

How can I pray for the right attitude as I suffer?
My suffering was good for me, for it taught me to pay attention to your decrees. Your instructions are more valuable to me than millions in gold and silver.

PSALM 119:71-72

Sometimes, suffering is so intense we can't feel anything except our pain. But God's Word gives us hope that our circumstances can become tools that shape and develop our character and help others going through similar circumstances. If your suffering causes you to doubt God's care for you, tell him how you feel. Write down your feelings and use them as a starting point for honest, vulnerable prayer today. How are you hoping God will redeem this hurt? This season?

YOU ARE WORTHY OF GOD'S LOVE

Lord, you say I am loved, but what if I don't feel lovable?

I have always loved you. I will always be your God. You know how much I love you, so put your trust in my love. I am love, and all who live in love live in me, and I live in them. Love has no fear, because perfect love expels all fear. If you are afraid, it is for fear of punishment, and this shows that you have not fully experienced my perfect love. Even if you feel guilty, I am greater than your feelings, and I know everything.

MALACHI 1:2; GENESIS 17:7; 1 JOHN 4:16, 18; 1 JOHN 3:20

Jesus, how can I live with an enduring sense that I am worthy of love?

I have loved you even as the Father has loved me. Remain in my love. When you obey my commandments, you remain in my love, just as I obey my Father and remain in his love. I have told you this so that you will be filled with my joy. Yes, your joy will overflow! For you know how dearly I love you, because I have given you the Holy Spirit to fill your heart with my love.

JOHN 15:9-11; ROMANS 5:5

What can I pray to be more aware of your love for me?

Lord, you take delight in me with gladness. With your love, you will calm all my fears. You will rejoice over me with joyful songs.

ZEPHANIAH 3:17

The greatest news of the gospel is that God's love is for everyone. Have you put your trust in his love? Can you trust God more than your feelings? Read Zephaniah 3:17 and soak in the assurances of his love: He delights in you, he calms your fears with his love, he rejoices in you, he sings songs over you. Repeat these truths today when you feel unlovable or unworthy of God's love.

A CRY FOR HELP

Lord, I've been praying for help, but nothing's changed. Can you hear me?

I am keeping you in my thoughts. I am your helper and your savior. My eyes watch over those who do right, and my ears are open to their prayers. In your distress, cry out to me; yes, cry to me for help. I will hear you from my sanctuary; your cry will reach my ears.

PSALM 40:17; I PETER 3:12; 2 SAMUEL 22:7

But if you hear me, where is the help I need?

Wait patiently for me. Be brave and courageous. Yes, wait patiently for me. The needy will not be ignored forever. Wait patiently, for it will surely take place. It will not be delayed. Come boldly to my throne, for I am your gracious God. There you will receive my mercy, and you will find grace to help you when you need it most. My grace is all you need.

PSALM 27:14; PSALM 9:18; HABAKKUK 2:3;
HEBREWS 4:16; 2 CORINTHIANS 12:9

What can I pray while I'm waiting
for you to help me?

I love you, LORD, because you hear my voice and my prayer for mercy. Because you bend down to listen, I will pray as long as I have breath! Listen to my voice in the morning, LORD. Each morning I bring my requests to you and wait expectantly.

PSALM 116:1-2; PSALM 5:3

Right now, stop and pray for five minutes. Tell God you are waiting for his help. While you pray, imagine God listening to you intently, as a loving father is attentive to his beloved child. Then take five minutes to listen to God. This exercise isn't meant to force God to speak but to open your heart to his voice.

THE KEY TO CONTROLLING YOUR ANGER

Lord, how can I better control my anger?
Don't sin by letting anger control you. Think about it overnight and remain silent. Sensible people control their temper; they earn respect by overlooking wrongs. You must be quick to listen, slow to speak, and slow to get angry.

PSALM 4:4; PROVERBS 19:11; JAMES 1:19

How can I be more gracious and compassionate?
I called you to do good, even if it means suffering, just as Christ suffered for you. He is your example, and you must follow in his steps. He did not retaliate when he was insulted, nor threaten revenge when he suffered. He left his case in my hands, and I always judge fairly. Be kind to each other, tenderhearted, forgiving one another, just as I through Christ have forgiven you.

I PETER 2:21, 23; EPHESIANS 4:32

What can I pray when I'm angry?

Lead me in the right path, O LORD, or my enemies will conquer me. Make your way plain for me to follow. I have hidden your word in my heart, that I might not sin against you.

PSALM 5:8; PSALM 119:11

Of all the emotions, anger is perhaps the most difficult to control. Anger itself is not wrong. God feels righteous anger. But anger becomes sin when we allow it to consume us, causing harm to our relationships with God and others. With which people, or in which circumstances, might God be calling you to be quick to listen, slow to speak, and slow to get angry? What are your anger triggers? How can you slow that moment down (e.g., use deep breathing, count to ten before speaking, ask the other person to explain his or her perspective)?

A FIRM FOUNDATION

Lord, what is the secret to a godly home?
Unless I build a house, the work of the builders is wasted. When you come to me, listen to my teaching, and then follow it. You are like a person building a house who digs deep and lays the foundation on solid rock. When the floodwaters rise and break against that house, it stands firm because it is well built.

PSALM 127:1; LUKE 6:47-48

What are some godly principles that will make my home well-built?
Love me with all your heart, all your soul, and all your strength. Commit yourself wholeheartedly to my commands. Tell future generations of my faithfulness to you. Direct your children onto the right path, and when they are older, they will not leave it. Discipline your children while there is hope. Otherwise, you will ruin their lives. Make allowance for each other's faults, and forgive anyone

who offends you. Clothe yourselves with love, which binds everyone together in perfect harmony.

DEUTERONOMY 6:5-6; ISAIAH 38:19;
PROVERBS 22:6; PROVERBS 19:18;
COLOSSIANS 3:13-14

What can I pray as I seek to build a godly home?
I will be careful to live a blameless life. I will lead a life of integrity in my own home. May the words of my mouth and the meditation of my heart be pleasing to you, O LORD, my rock and my redeemer.

PSALM 101:2; PSALM 19:14

Go through your house and pray that God would be present, helping you to use your home to love him and others well. Pray that God would remind you to build your house upon his principles, honoring him in all you do and say.

MAKE THE MOST OF WHAT YOU ARE GIVEN

Lord, how can I take good care of
what you've given me?

The Kingdom of Heaven can be illustrated by the story of a man going on a trip. He called together his servants and entrusted his money to them while he was gone. He gave five bags of silver to one, two bags of silver to another, and one bag of silver to the last—dividing it in proportion to their abilities. To those who use well what they are given, even more will be given, and they will have an abundance. But from those who do nothing, even what little they have will be taken away.

MATTHEW 25:14-15, 29

What are practical ways I can
best use what I have?

Honor me with your wealth and with the best part of everything you produce. If you have two shirts, give one to the poor. If you have food, share it with those who are hungry. When God's people are in need, be ready to help them. Always be eager to practice hospitality.

PROVERBS 3:9; LUKE 3:11; ROMANS 12:13

What can I pray when it feels hard to be generous with my time and resources?
O LORD God, the heavens are yours, and the earth is yours; everything in the world is yours—you created it all.

PSALM 89:8, 11

Stewardship acknowledges that everything we have is a gift from God. What has God blessed you with? Time? Energy? Wealth? Special talents? Today, reflect on this question: How can I make the best possible use of what God has given me in order to make the greatest possible impact for him?

CELEBRATE GOD'S PRESENCE

Lord, what is the secret to a joyful life?

All who seek me will praise me. Your heart will rejoice with everlasting joy. Joyful are those who have me as their helper, whose hope is in me. I am always with you. No wonder your heart is glad, and you rejoice.

PSALM 22:26; PSALM 146:5; PSALM 16:8-9

If your presence brings joy, what about the seasons of life when I don't feel joyful?

Don't be surprised at the fiery trials you are going through, as if something strange were happening to you. Instead, be very glad—for these trials make you partners with Christ in his suffering, so that you will have the wonderful joy of seeing his glory when it is revealed to all the world.

1 PETER 4:12-13

What can I pray to find joy in your presence?
How lovely is your dwelling place, O LORD of Heaven's Armies. With my whole being, body and soul, I will shout joyfully to you, the living God. O Lord, you are so good, so ready to forgive, so full of unfailing love for all who ask for your help. Give me happiness, O Lord, for I give myself to you.

PSALM 84:1-2; PSALM 86:5; PSALM 86:4

Joy is the celebration of your friendship with God. Feelings and circumstances can't determine your sense of joy. Even in times of trouble and anguish, you can experience joy because of God's unfailing love for you. What is one reason you can celebrate God's presence with you? Take five minutes to celebrate this today. Take a praise walk, enjoy a special meal, journal your gratitude, or give yourself a small present as a reminder that God's presence is a continual gift of joy.

THINK OF YOURSELF LESS

Lord, what does true humility look like?

You must have the same attitude that Christ Jesus had. Though he and I are one, he did not think of equality with me as something to cling to. Instead, he gave up his divine privileges; he took the humble position of a slave and was born as a human being. When he appeared in human form, he humbled himself in obedience to me and died a criminal's death on a cross.

PHILIPPIANS 2:5-8

How can I grow in humility?

Don't think you are better than you really are. Be honest in your evaluation of yourself, measuring yourself by the faith I have given you. Don't be selfish; don't try to impress others. Be humble, thinking of others as better than yourself. I must become greater and greater, and you must become less and less.

ROMANS 12:3; PHILIPPIANS 2:3; JOHN 3:30

What can I pray to grow in humility?

When I look at the night sky and see the work of your fingers—the moon and the stars you set in place—what are mere mortals that you should think about them, human beings that you should care for them? Teach me your ways, O LORD, that I may live according to your truth! Grant me purity of heart, so that I may honor you. Bend down, O LORD, and hear my prayer; answer me, for I need your help.

PSALM 8:3-4; PSALM 86:11; PSALM 86:1

C. S. Lewis once said, "If anyone would like to acquire humility, . . . the first step is to realise that one is proud." Take notice today of how often you think of yourself or try to project a certain image to others. Ask the Holy Spirit to reveal when you are thinking too much about yourself. What would it look like for you to become more focused on others?

YOU HAVE PERMISSION TO ENJOY LIFE!

Lord, what is the proper balance between work and leisure?

Never be lazy, but work hard and serve me enthusiastically. Work willingly at whatever you do, as though you were working for me rather than for people. Then you will get the satisfaction of a job well done. It is good for people to eat, drink, and enjoy their work under the sun. To enjoy your work and accept your lot in life—this is indeed a gift from me.

ROMANS 12:11; COLOSSIANS 3:23; GALATIANS 6:4;
ECCLESIASTES 5:18-19

So is it okay to have times of leisure and fun?

Who can eat or enjoy anything apart from me? Whatever is good and perfect is a gift coming down to you from me. There is nothing better for people in this world than to eat, drink, and enjoy life. That way you will experience some happiness along with all the hard work I give you under the sun.

ECCLESIASTES 2:25; JAMES 1:17; ECCLESIASTES 8:15

*What can I pray that will remind me
to take time to enjoy life?*

How joyful are those who fear you, Lord—all who follow your ways! We will enjoy the fruit of our labor. How joyful and prosperous we will be! Let us rejoice. Let us be glad in your presence. Let us be filled with joy.

PSALM 128:1-2; PSALM 68:3

How does God's Word encourage you to balance your work and play? Think about last week. When did you feel most productive? When did you feel tired or burned out? What activities refreshed you? Is there a way you can bring times of rest and refreshment into your schedule before you reach the point of exhaustion? Schedule a life-giving activity into your upcoming week. Write it on the calendar so you don't forget.

WHAT BRINGS GOD JOY

Lord, what brings you joy?

My delight is in those who fear me, those who put their hope in my unfailing love. Don't let the wise boast in their wisdom, or the powerful boast in their power, or the rich boast in their riches. But those who wish to boast should boast in this alone: that they truly know me and understand that I am the LORD who demonstrates unfailing love and who brings justice and righteousness to the earth, and that I delight in these things.

PSALM 147:11; JEREMIAH 9:23-24

How can I live this way?

The highest heavens and the earth and everything in it all belong to me. Yet I chose you. I restore the crushed spirit of the humble and revive the courage of those with repentant hearts. I require only that you fear me, and live in a way that pleases me, and love me and serve me with all your heart and soul. I have told you what is good, and this is what

I require of you: to do what is right, to love mercy, and to walk humbly with me.

DEUTERONOMY 10:14-15; ISAIAH 57:15; DEUTERONOMY 10:12; MICAH 6:8

What can I pray to focus on bringing you joy?
May I show love to you, LORD, by walking in your ways and holding tightly to you.

DEUTERONOMY 11:22

God delights in you because you are his child. What thrills his heart most is when his children love him back. Today, try to focus on living in a way that pleases the Lord. Some examples might be choosing to praise him in the midst of navigating pain or difficulty, showing mercy, or expressing gratitude for his unfailing love for you.

THE POWER OF WORDS

Lord, is gossip really that bad?

A tiny spark can set a great forest on fire. And among all the parts of the body, the tongue is a flame of fire. Sometimes it praises me, and sometimes it curses those who have been made in my image. Do not spread slanderous gossip. Rumors are dainty morsels that sink deep into one's heart. A troublemaker plants seeds of strife; gossip separates the best of friends.

JAMES 3:5-6, 9; LEVITICUS 19:16;
PROVERBS 18:8; PROVERBS 16:28

*How can I talk about others in a way
that pleases you?*

Let everything you say be good and helpful, so that your words will be an encouragement to those who hear them. And whatever you do or say, let it be as a representative of the Lord Jesus. Judge fairly, and show mercy and kindness to one another. Be tenderhearted, and keep a humble attitude. Don't repay evil for evil. Don't retaliate with insults when people insult you. Instead, pay them back with a blessing. That is what I have called you to do, and I will grant you my blessing.

EPHESIANS 4:29; COLOSSIANS 3:17;
ZECHARIAH 7:9; I PETER 3:8-9

What can I pray when I'm tempted to gossip?
Take control of what I say, O LORD, and guard my lips.

PSALM 141:3

Our words hold great power—even the ones we say behind someone's back. Words always have consequences, sometimes to others and sometimes to our own hearts. Take time to pray over these questions: Are my words kind, encouraging, true, and necessary? When am I most tempted to gossip? Who am I most tempted to gossip about? Pray over those situations and people right now—asking God to help you control your tongue and change your heart.

SPEAK UP FOR THE VULNERABLE

Lord, sometimes the world seems so unfair.
Will your justice really prevail?

Let the fields and their crops burst out with joy! Let the trees of the forest sing for joy before me, for I am coming! I am coming to judge the earth. I will judge the world with justice, and the nations with my truth. The godly will rejoice when they see injustice avenged. Then at last everyone will say, "There truly is a reward for those who live for God; surely there is a God who judges justly here on earth."

PSALM 96:12-13; PSALM 58:10-11

What can I do to promote a more just world?

Give justice to the poor and the orphan; uphold the rights of the oppressed and the destitute. Rescue the poor and helpless; deliver them from the grasp of evil people. Speak up for those who cannot speak for themselves; ensure justice for those being crushed. Yes, speak up for the poor and helpless, and see that they get justice.

PSALM 82:3-4; PROVERBS 31:8-9

What can I pray when I see injustice in the world?
Lord, you reign forever, executing judgment from
your throne. You will judge the world with justice and
rule the nations with fairness. You are a shelter for the
oppressed, a refuge in times of trouble. Those who
know your name trust in you, for you, O Lord, do
not abandon those who search for you.

PSALM 9:7-10

*What injustices stir your heart to action? What brokenness in the world
moves you to compassion? Find a way to get involved. It might be choosing
to buy fair-trade fashions or coffee, supporting an organization that works
for social justice, going on a mission trip, volunteering with children with
special needs, or sponsoring a child in a developing country.*

YOU ARE NEVER REALLY STUCK

Lord, I feel stuck in a bad situation.
Can you help me?

Search for me and for my strength; continually seek me. Remember the wonders I have performed, my miracles, and the rulings I have given. Don't be afraid, for I am with you. Don't be discouraged, for I am your God. I will strengthen you and help you. I will hold you up with my victorious right hand.

I CHRONICLES 16:11; PSALM 105:5;
ISAIAH 41:10

But, Lord, it feels impossible
to get out of this . . .

Humanly speaking, it is impossible. But with me everything is possible. You don't have enough faith. I tell you the truth, if you had faith even as small as a mustard seed, you could say to this mountain, "Move from here to there," and it would move. Nothing would be impossible.

MATTHEW 19:26; MATTHEW 17:20

What can I pray when I feel unable to cope?
I recall all you have done, O Lord; I remember your
wonderful deeds of long ago. They are constantly
in my thoughts. I cannot stop thinking about your
mighty works. O God, your ways are holy. Is there
any god as mighty as you? You are the God of great
wonders!

PSALM 77:11-14

The Bible is full of stories in which God helps his people out of impossible situations. The mighty God of the universe is able to provide a way out where it seems as if there is no escape. When the circumstances of life make you feel trapped and discouraged, the best thing to do is to remember God's unlimited resources. Meditate on Exodus 14, Daniel 3, and Acts 16:16-40. How do these stories bring hope that God can rescue you from your circumstances?

GOD SEES YOUR TEARS

Lord, how can I find comfort when I cry alone?
I am your merciful Father and the source of all comfort. I am close to the brokenhearted; I rescue those whose spirits are crushed. Pour out your heart to me. Pray about everything. Tell me what you need, and thank me for all I have done. Then you will experience my peace, which exceeds anything you can understand. My peace will guard your heart and mind.

2 CORINTHIANS 1:3; PSALM 34:18; PSALM 62:8;
PHILIPPIANS 4:6-7

*How can I know you care about
the things I cry over?*
I am like a father to my children, tender and compassionate to those who fear me. For I know how weak you are. And the Holy Spirit helps you in your weakness. For example, you don't know what I want you to pray for. But the Holy Spirit prays for you with groanings that cannot be expressed in words.

PSALM 103:13-14; ROMANS 8:26

In the midst of my tears, what can I pray to remind myself that you are with me?

You keep track of all my sorrows. You have collected all my tears in your bottle. You have recorded each one in your book. You are the God who sees me.

PSALM 56:8; GENESIS 16:13

Crying all by yourself is one of the most humbling and lonely experiences in life. However, even when you feel most alone, God is with you, holding you in that moment. His Word says he cares so much about your tears that he catches each one. Write out the prayer above and put it in a place where you often cry alone. The next time you need to be reminded of this truth, read this prayer, and remember that you are never alone.

THE IMPORTANCE OF LOYALTY TO GOD

Lord, what does loyalty to you look like?

Do not make idols of any shape or form. Love me with all your heart, all your soul, and all your strength. Commit yourself wholeheartedly to these commands that I am giving you. Come, follow me. If you refuse to take up your cross and follow me, you are not worthy of being mine. If you cling to your life, you will lose it; but if you give up your life for me, you will find it. I protect those who are loyal to me.

DEUTERONOMY 4:23; DEUTERONOMY 6:5-6;
MATTHEW 4:19; MATTHEW 10:38-39;
PSALM 31:23

What does disloyalty to you look like?

Idols are merely things of silver and gold, shaped by human hands. They have mouths but cannot speak, and eyes but cannot see. They have ears but cannot hear, and noses but cannot smell. Repent and turn away from your idols. You have abandoned me and turned your back on me. Do not let sin control the way you live; do not give in to sinful desires. Do not let any part of your body become an instrument of evil to serve sin.

PSALM 115:4-6; EZEKIEL 14:6; JEREMIAH 15:6; ROMANS 6:12-13

What can I pray to renew my loyalty to you?
I've promised it once, and I'll promise it again: I will obey your righteous regulations. Not to me, O LORD, not to me, but to your name goes all the glory for your unfailing love and faithfulness.

PSALM 119:106; PSALM 115:1

Reflect on the following questions: Are there idols in my life? What am I most devoted to (family, friends, appearance, money, health, security, success, control)? Consider some of the characteristics of idols (speechless, blind, deaf, senseless, unfeeling, directionless, lifeless). The Bible warns that those who trust in idols become just like them. Ask the Holy Spirit to convict you if you are disloyal to God in some area. Pray the prayer above to recommit your loyalty and devotion to God alone.

EXPERIENCE MORE OF GOD

Lord, how can I have more of you in my life?

Come to me with your ears wide open. Listen, and
you will find life. I am good to those who depend on
me, to those who search for me. My purpose is for the
nations to seek after me and perhaps feel their way
toward me and find me—though I am not far from
any one of you. I will be found by you.

ISAIAH 55:3; LAMENTATIONS 3:25; ACTS 17:27;
JEREMIAH 29:14

Will you help me find you?

I am working in you, giving you the desire and the
power to do what pleases me. And if you search for
me with all your heart and soul, you will find me.
Do not be afraid or discouraged, for I will be with
you; I will neither fail you nor abandon you.

PHILIPPIANS 2:13; DEUTERONOMY 4:29;
DEUTERONOMY 31:8

*What can I pray when it feels like
you are far away?*

LORD, you are close to all who call on you, yes, to
all who call on you in truth. You grant the desires of
those who fear you; you hear their cries for help and
rescue them.

PSALM 145:18-19

*Every believer experiences seasons when God feels far away, and maybe even
nonexistent. In those times, we must rely more on the truth of God's promises than
on the strength of our feelings. Do you strive to have a pure heart? Do you obey
God's commandments? If you can answer yes to these questions, God promises you
will experience more of him. Remember that God is with you wherever you are.*

He sees you, and he is working in your heart to draw you closer to himself.

WHAT GETS IN THE WAY
OF KNOWING GOD?

*Lord, what are some obstacles to
deepening my faith in you?*

Do not love this world nor the things it offers you.
For the world offers only a craving for physical pleasure, a craving for everything you see, and pride in
your achievements and possessions. These are not
from me, but are from this world. And this world
is fading away, along with everything that people
crave. But anyone who does what pleases me will
live forever.

I JOHN 2:15-17

*So how can I avoid these obstacles and
live for what will last?*

Don't slip back into your old ways of living to satisfy
your own desires. Don't envy violent people or copy
their ways. Such wicked people are detestable to me,
but I offer my friendship to the godly. Don't copy
the behavior and customs of this world, but let me

transform you into a new person by changing the way
you think. Then you will learn to know my will for
you, which is good and pleasing and perfect.

1 PETER 1:14; PROVERBS 3:31-32; ROMANS 12:2

*What can I pray when I encounter barriers
to a deeper relationship with you?*
LORD, you are a friend to those who fear you. You teach
them your covenant. My eyes are always on you, for
you rescue me from the traps of my enemies.

PSALM 25:14-15

*What cravings or distractions are your biggest obstacles to going deep
with God? How might social media affect your desires? Keep a journal today
of where your thoughts go after you spend time watching TV or using
social media. Are you left craving newer or better things or coveting someone else's life? Are you distracted from what is good, pure, and true?
Review your journal prayerfully at the end of the day.*

HOW TO KNOW WHAT IS TRULY BEST FOR YOU

Lord, how could you close a door on something I so badly wanted?

My thoughts are nothing like your thoughts, and my ways are far beyond anything you could imagine. For I am about to do something new. See, I have already begun! Do you not see it? I will make a pathway through the wilderness. I will cause everything to work together for the good of those who love me and are called according to my purpose.

ISAIAH 55:8; ISAIAH 43:19; ROMANS 8:28

Lord, is there a story from your Word to encourage me to be open to your plan?

Paul and Silas traveled through the area of Phrygia and Galatia, because the Holy Spirit had prevented them from preaching the word in the province of Asia at that time. They headed north for the province of Bithynia, but again the Spirit of Jesus did not let them go there. That night, Paul had a vision. A man from northern Greece was pleading with him, "Come over to Macedonia and help us!" So they decided to leave at once, having concluded that I was calling them to preach the Good News there.

ACTS 16:6-10

*What can I pray when I feel discouraged
by a closed door?*
Show me the right path, O Lord; point out the road for me to follow. Show me where to walk, for I give myself to you. Fill me completely with joy and peace because I trust in you. Then I will overflow with confident hope through the power of the Holy Spirit.

PSALM 25:4; PSALM 143:8; ROMANS 15:13

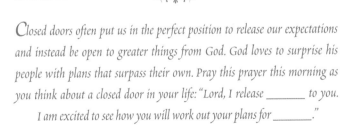

Closed doors often put us in the perfect position to release our expectations and instead be open to greater things from God. God loves to surprise his people with plans that surpass their own. Pray this prayer this morning as you think about a closed door in your life: "Lord, I release _____ to you. I am excited to see how you will work out your plans for _____."

THE PURPOSE
OF GOD'S BLESSINGS

Lord, how can I use what I have to help others?
When my people are in need, be ready to help them.
Always be eager to practice hospitality. If you have
enough money to live well and see a brother or sister
in need but show no compassion—how can my love
be in you? Dear child, don't merely say that you love
others; show the truth by your actions.

ROMANS 12:13; 1 JOHN 3:17-18

What is the impact of giving freely?
I love a person who gives cheerfully. I will generously
provide all you need. Then you will always have everything you need and plenty left over to share with
others. As the Scriptures say, "They share freely and
give generously to the poor. Their good deeds will be
remembered forever." For I am the one who provides
seed for the farmer and then bread to eat. In the same
way, I will provide and increase your resources and
then produce a great harvest of generosity in you.

2 CORINTHIANS 9:7-10

What can I pray when I want to
develop a generous spirit?

Lord, may you make my love for others and for all
people grow and overflow, just as my love for you
overflows. May you, as a result, make my heart strong,
blameless, and holy as I stand before you when my
Lord Jesus comes again with all his holy people.

1 THESSALONIANS 3:12-13

*God blesses you so his blessings can flow through you into the lives of others.
When you open your hands and give generously, you're also emptying your
hands to receive from God. The next time someone compliments something of
yours, consider giving it to him or her. What does it feel like to give so freely?*

YOU CAN NEVER
DRIFT TOO FAR

Lord, I have drifted so far from my faith.
How can you accept me again?

If a man has a hundred sheep and one of them gets
lost, what will he do? Won't he leave the ninety-nine
others in the wilderness and go to search for the
one that is lost until he finds it? And when he has
found it, he will joyfully carry it home on his shoul-
ders. There is more joy in heaven over one lost sinner
who repents and returns to me than over ninety-nine
others who are righteous and haven't strayed away!

LUKE 15:4-5, 7

How can I come close to you again?

Return to me, the LORD your God, for your sins have
brought you down. Bring your confessions, and return
to me. Say to me, "Forgive all my sins and graciously
receive me." Then I will heal you of your faithless-
ness; my love will know no bounds, for my anger will
be gone forever.

HOSEA 14:1-2, 4

What can I pray when I find myself drifting again?
Restore to me the joy of your salvation, and make me
willing to obey you. The sacrifice you desire is a broken spirit. You will not reject a broken and repentant
heart, O God.

PSALM 51:12, 17

*No matter how far we have drifted from God, there is no amount of distance
he won't cross to bring us back. And his Word assures us that when we repent
and return to him, he responds with joy and celebration. Take a minute to
confess any hidden sin or resistance toward God. Now imagine him responding
the way the shepherd responds in Luke 15. How does this make you feel?*

HOW RELIABLE ARE YOU?

What is an example from your Word of someone who was trustworthy?

The money brought to the Temple was not used for making silver bowls, lamp snuffers, basins, trumpets, or other articles of gold or silver for my Temple. It was paid to the workmen, who used it for the Temple repairs. No accounting of this money was required from the construction supervisors, because they were honest and trustworthy men.

2 KINGS 12:13-15

What principles from your Word develop trustworthy character?

And now, what do I require of you? I require only that you fear me, the LORD your God, and live in a way that pleases me, and love me and serve me with all your heart and soul. A gossip goes around telling secrets, but those who are trustworthy can keep a confidence. The trustworthy person will get a rich reward, but a person who wants quick riches will get into trouble. Don't plot harm against your neighbor. Tell the truth to each other. Render verdicts in your courts that are just and that lead to peace. Don't scheme against each other.

DEUTERONOMY 10:12; PROVERBS 11:13; PROVERBS 28:20; PROVERBS 3:29; ZECHARIAH 8:16-17

What can I pray to help me grow into a more trustworthy person?

Lord, help me to do things in such a way that everyone can see I am honorable. Give me understanding and I will obey your instructions; I will put them into practice with all my heart. Make me walk along the path of your commands, for that is where my happiness is found. Give me an eagerness for your laws rather than a love for money!

ROMANS 12:17; PSALM 119:34-36

Who in your life has proven reliable? What characteristics make them trustworthy? Today, write an email or send a text thanking them for being an example of honorable character in your life. Then ask them what you can do to grow in trustworthiness. Be open to advice.

PERFECT PEACE

Lord, how can I experience a greater sense of peace?
Fix your thoughts on what is true, and honorable,
and right, and pure, and lovely, and admirable. Think
about things that are excellent and worthy of praise.
Keep putting into practice all you learned and received
from me—everything you heard from me and saw me
doing. I will keep in perfect peace all who trust in me,
all whose thoughts are fixed on me!

PHILIPPIANS 4:8-9; ISAIAH 26:3

*What does it look like to keep my mind fixed
on positive thoughts?*
Don't worry about anything; instead, pray about
everything. Tell me what you need, and thank me
for all I have done. Then you will experience my
peace, which exceeds anything you can understand.
My peace will guard your heart and mind as you
live in Christ Jesus.

PHILIPPIANS 4:6-7

*What can I pray to ask for your peace
in any circumstance?*

May you, the Lord of peace himself, give me your
peace at all times and in every situation. May you
equip me with all I need for doing your will. May
you produce in me, through the power of Jesus
Christ, every good thing that is pleasing to you.
And let the peace that comes from Christ rule in
my heart.

2 THESSALONIANS 3:16; HEBREWS 13:21;
COLOSSIANS 3:15

---

*What is disrupting your peace right now? Reread Philippians 4:6-7. You
can keep your thoughts focused on God by choosing prayer over worry, telling God all of your cares and needs, and thanking him for what he's done in
the past. Focusing on God won't eliminate the troubles from your life, but it
will cultivate trust in his care. Use this model in your prayer time today,
asking God to exchange his peace for your worries.*

RELEASE YOUR NEED FOR APPROVAL

Lord, how do I balance my desire for your approval with my desire for the approval of others?
Seek my Kingdom above all else, and live righteously. For my Kingdom is not a matter of what you eat or drink, but of living a life of goodness and peace and joy in the Holy Spirit. If you serve Christ with this attitude, you will please me, and others will approve of you, too.

MATTHEW 6:33; ROMANS 14:17-18

How can I earn a good reputation?
Never let loyalty and kindness leave you! Tie them around your neck as a reminder. Write them deep within your heart. Then you will find favor with both me and people, and you will earn a good reputation.

PROVERBS 3:3-4

What can I pray when I find myself putting others' approval above God's?

I'm not trying to win the approval of people, but of you, God. If pleasing people were my goal, I would not be your servant. For I am not ashamed of this Good News about Christ. O LORD my God, you alone are the one I worship. I will praise you, LORD, with all my heart.

GALATIANS 1:10; ROMANS 1:16; ISAIAH 26:13; PSALM 9:1

*M*ost people have a deep need to be liked and approved of by others. This isn't necessarily a bad thing, but this desire becomes distorted when we allow the opinions of others to define us. When you put Christ's Kingdom first, other people's approval is put into proper perspective. Oftentimes, others will be drawn to you because of your kindness, loyalty, and love. In what ways have you put the approval of others before God? Confess this to him and receive his forgiveness.

GOD'S POWER AT WORK WITHIN YOU

*Lord, what does it mean that I have power
as a follower of Christ?*

I am working in you, giving you the desire and the
power to do what pleases me. I give power to the weak
and strength to the powerless. With my help you will
do mighty things. I am able, through my mighty power
at work within you, to accomplish infinitely more than
you might ask or think. This is the same mighty power
that raised Christ from the dead and seated him in the
place of honor at my right hand in the heavenly realms.

PHILIPPIANS 2:13; ISAIAH 40:29; PSALM 60:12;
EPHESIANS 3:20; EPHESIANS 1:19-20

How do I experience this power?

This is the secret: Christ lives in you. The Spirit who
lives in you is greater than the spirit who lives in the
world. From my glorious, unlimited resources I will
empower you with inner strength through my Spirit.

COLOSSIANS 1:27; 1 JOHN 4:4; EPHESIANS 3:16

*What can I pray to understand the greatness
of your power within me?*

Lord, I pray that I will understand the incredible greatness of your power for those who believe you. I know
that you will answer me from your holy heaven and
rescue me by your great power. For you are working
in me, giving me the desire and the power to do what
pleases you.

EPHESIANS 1:19; PSALM 20:6; PHILIPPIANS 2:13

*God's power—the wisdom that formed the world and the strength that
raised Jesus from the dead—is available to you! Think about your biggest
challenge right now. Write down what you think would be the best outcome
of this situation. What do you hope for? What feels impossible to ask?
Tuck the list in your Bible as a sign that you are giving this challenge
to God—trusting that by his mighty power at work within you, he is
able to do infinitely more than you might ask or imagine.*

THE CHOICE IS YOURS

What is the secret to having a cheerful attitude even during hard times?

Trust in my unfailing love. Rejoice because I have rescued you. Sing to me because I am good to you. Let the heavens be glad, and the earth rejoice! Tell all the nations, "The LORD reigns!" Let the sea and everything in it shout praise! Give thanks to me, for I am good! Always be full of joy in me. I say it again—rejoice!

PSALM 13:5-6; 1 CHRONICLES 16:31-32, 34; PHILIPPIANS 4:4

Lord Jesus, what can help me stay cheerful?

Be glad and rejoice in my unfailing love, for I have seen your troubles, and I care about the anguish of your soul. The humble will see me at work and be glad. Let all who seek my help be encouraged. I have loved you even as the Father has loved me. Remain in my love. When you obey my commandments, you remain in my love, just as I obey my Father's commandments and remain in his love. I have told you these things so that you will be filled with my joy. Yes, your joy will overflow!

PSALM 31:7; PSALM 69:32; JOHN 15:9-11

What can I pray when I find my attitude becoming negative?

Praise the LORD! Praise God in his sanctuary; praise him in his mighty heaven! Praise him for his mighty works; praise his unequaled greatness! Let everything that breathes sing praises to the LORD! Praise the LORD!

PSALM 150:1-2, 6

Gratitude lifts up the soul. Meditating on God's goodness and sovereign plan reminds us of his abundant grace and unfailing love for those who follow him. We cannot control what happens to us, but we can control how we respond to it. God's Word affirms the power of gratitude and encourages us to watch for the ways God is working. What is a negative thought you've been dwelling on lately? (For example, "I'm not good enough.") Can you reframe your thinking to rejoice in what God says about you?

BE A LIGHT IN THIS DARK WORLD

*Lord, how should following you affect the way
I engage with culture?*

You are the light of the world. Let your good deeds
shine out for all to see, so that everyone will praise
me. Love each other. Just as I have loved you, you
should love each other. Your love for one another
will prove to the world that you are my disciples.

MATTHEW 5:14, 16; JOHN 13:34-35

*How can I respond when society isolates me
for following you?*

Bless those who persecute you. Don't curse them;
pray that I will bless them. Never pay back evil with
more evil. Never take revenge. Leave that to my
righteous anger. Instead, do what the Scriptures say:
"If your enemies are hungry, feed them. If they are
thirsty, give them something to drink. In doing this,
you will heap burning coals of shame on their heads."

ROMANS 12:14, 17, 19-20

What can I pray as I seek to live a godly life in this culture?

I'm not asking you to take me out of the world, Lord Jesus, but to keep me safe from the evil one. Make me holy by your truth; teach me your word, which is truth.

JOHN 17:15, 17

The life of a believer can be summed up in two commands: love God and love others. That is your call and challenge in today's society. If you are truly following Jesus, you will at some point be misunderstood, ridiculed, shamed, and possibly even persecuted. No matter how others respond to your faith, choose to stand strong and confidently continue to love others. What can you do today to intentionally love someone around you who may not know Jesus?

BEAR THIS KIND
OF FRUIT

What is the fruit of the Spirit? Why is it important?
Let the Holy Spirit guide your life. Then you won't be
doing what your sinful nature craves. When you are
directed by the Spirit, the Holy Spirit produces this
kind of fruit in your life: love, joy, peace, patience,
kindness, goodness, faithfulness, gentleness, and
self-control.

GALATIANS 5:16, 18, 22-23

Lord, how can I develop these character qualities?
Remain in me, and I will remain in you. For a branch
cannot produce fruit if it is severed from the vine, and
you cannot be fruitful unless you remain in me. Grow
in my grace and the knowledge of me. Delight in my
law, meditating on it day and night. You will be like
a tree planted along the riverbank, bearing fruit each
season, and you will prosper in all you do.

JOHN 15:4; 2 PETER 3:18; PSALM 1:2-3

*How can I pray for you to reveal which fruits
need to mature in my life?*

God, I ask you to give me complete knowledge of
your will and to give me spiritual wisdom and understanding. Then the way I live will always honor and
please you, and my life will produce every kind of
good fruit.

COLOSSIANS 1:9-10

*The fruit of the Spirit is the result of maturity and growth in your
relationship with Jesus. The more you strive to know God and live life with
him, the more evident these fruits will become in you. Consider each fruit of
the Spirit one by one: love, joy, peace, patience, kindness, goodness, faithfulness, gentleness, and self-control. Which specific fruit might God be trying to bring to maturity in you? What current circumstances might God
be using to help you grow more fruitful in this area?*

GROWING MORE STEADY AND CONFIDENT

Lord, how can I feel secure and steady despite life's twists and turns?

How joyful are those who fear me and delight in obeying my commands. Such people do not fear bad news; they confidently trust me to care for them. They will no longer be immature like children. They won't be tossed and blown about by every wind of new teaching. Instead, they will speak the truth in love, growing in every way more and more like Christ.

PSALM 112:1, 6-7; EPHESIANS 4:14-15

How can I develop deeper confidence in you?

Anyone who listens to my teaching and follows it is wise, like a person who builds a house on solid rock. Though the rain comes in torrents and the flood-waters rise and the winds beat against that house, it won't collapse, because it is built on bedrock. Trust in me always, for I am the eternal Rock.

MATTHEW 7:24-25; ISAIAH 26:4

*How can I pray for a strong foundation
that is built on trust in you?*

Teach me to do your will, for you are my God. May
your gracious Spirit lead me forward on a firm footing.

PSALM 143:10

*God promises that those who trust in him will experience joy and confidence
even when life feels overwhelming. Do you long for this kind of stability? God's
unchanging eternal nature is a firm foundation—the most secure place to anchor
your hope. Are there places where your foundation isn't solidly attached to the
Lord? What are the rains, winds, and floodwaters in this season of life that make
you feel unsteady? Ask the Lord this morning how you can be more like the house
that won't collapse—one with a foundation built on the eternal Rock.*

PRAY FOR YOUR COMMUNITY

Lord, what is my responsibility to my community?
Work for the peace and prosperity of the city where
I sent you. Pray for it, for its welfare will determine
your welfare.

JEREMIAH 29:7

What can I do for my community?
Pray for all people. Ask me to help them; intercede
on their behalf, and give thanks for them. Pray this
way for all who are in authority so that you can live a
peaceful and quiet life marked by godliness and dig-
nity. This is good and pleases me, for I want everyone
to be saved and to understand the truth.

I TIMOTHY 2:1-4

What can I pray to intercede for my neighbors?
I have not stopped thanking you for them. I pray for
them constantly, asking you, the glorious Father of my
Lord Jesus Christ, to give them spiritual wisdom and

insight so that they might grow in their knowledge of you. I pray that their hearts will be flooded with light so that they can understand the confident hope you have given to those you called—your holy people who are your rich and glorious inheritance. I also pray that they will understand the incredible greatness of your power for those who believe you.

EPHESIANS 1:16-19

Have you ever considered that God has placed you where you are because it is where you can have the greatest impact for him? Are you in tune with the conversations and needs of your community? One way to have an impact is through prayer. Set a timer on your phone today to remind you to spend five minutes in prayer for the city where you live. Use the prayer above or voice your own.

MAKE THE MOST OF EVERY OPPORTUNITY

Lord, how does being faithful to your principles create doors of opportunity?

Those who live to please the Spirit will harvest everlasting life from the Spirit. So don't get tired of doing what is good. At just the right time you will reap a harvest of blessing if you don't give up. Whenever you have the opportunity, you should do good to everyone—especially to those in the family of faith.

GALATIANS 6:8-10

Lord Jesus, what opportunities do I have to show my faithfulness to you?

I was hungry, and you fed me. I was thirsty, and you gave me a drink. I was a stranger, and you invited me into your home. I was naked, and you gave me clothing. I was sick, and you cared for me. I was in prison, and you visited me. I tell you the truth, when you did it to one of the least of these my brothers and sisters, you were doing it to me!

MATTHEW 25:35-36, 40

What can I pray when I want to seize opportunities to be faithful to you?

Help me not to get tired of doing what is good, Lord. When your people are in need, may I be ready to help them. Let me always be eager to practice hospitality. May I be happy with those who are happy, and weep with those who weep. May I always be filled with the fruit of my salvation—the righteous character produced in my life by Jesus Christ.

GALATIANS 6:9; ROMANS 12:13, 15; PHILIPPIANS 1:11

Each new day brings opportunities to show faithfulness to the Lord. Read the passages above for some practical ideas for showing your loyalty to him. Pick one to do today. Can you provide a meal or clothing for someone? Offer friendship? Care for someone who is sick? Donate to a pressing need in the world? Pray that this act of faithfulness will open doors for the gospel in the life of the one you serve.

BUILD EACH OTHER UP

Lord, what is the key to building strong relationships with other believers?

You say, "I am allowed to do anything"—but not everything is good for you. You say, "I am allowed to do anything"—but not everything is beneficial. Don't be concerned for your own good but for the good of others. You must not just please yourself. You should help others do what is right and build them up in me.

I CORINTHIANS 10:23-24; ROMANS 15:1-2

How can I build up other believers?

Sympathize with each other. Love each other as brothers and sisters. Be tenderhearted, and keep a humble attitude. Warn those who are lazy. Encourage those who are timid. Take tender care of those who are weak. Be patient with everyone. See that no one pays back evil for evil, but always try to do good to each other and to all people. Always be joyful. Never stop praying. Be thankful in all circumstances, for this is my will for you who belong to Christ Jesus.

I PETER 3:8; I THESSALONIANS 5:14-18

What can I pray about my relationships?

God, who gives patience and encouragement, help me live in complete harmony with others, as is fitting for your followers. Then we can join together with one voice, giving praise and glory to you, the Father of our Lord Jesus Christ.

ROMANS 15:5-6

Do you know someone who is good at encouraging others? Investing in other believers means thinking about what is helpful to them. Others are built up when you show the same love and thoughtfulness that Christ shows you. What is a step you can take today to invest in another believer? Is there someone you can mentor? A person you can pray for? Someone who needs to receive an encouraging text or email?

TREAT OTHERS HOW YOU WANT TO BE TREATED

Lord, what does your Word say about judging others?
Do not judge others, and you will not be judged. For you
will be treated as you treat others. The standard you use
in judging is the standard by which you will be judged.
Do not twist justice by favoring the poor or being par-
tial to the rich and powerful. Always judge people fairly.
Don't make judgments about anyone ahead of time—
before Jesus returns. For he will bring your darkest secrets
to light and will reveal your private motives. Then I will
give to each one whatever praise is due.

MATTHEW 7:1-2; LEVITICUS 19:15;
1 CORINTHIANS 4:5

What perspective should guide the way I see others?
Do not condemn others, or it will all come back
against you. Forgive others, and you will be forgiven.
Why worry about a speck in your friend's eye when
you have a log in your own? How can you think of
saying, "Friend, let me help you get rid of that speck

in your eye," when you can't see past the log in your own eye? First get rid of the log in your own eye; then you will see well enough to deal with the speck in your friend's eye. Make allowance for each other's faults, and forgive anyone who offends you. Remember, the Lord forgave you, so you must forgive others.

LUKE 6:37, 41-42; COLOSSIANS 3:13

What can I pray when I feel tempted to judge others?
Everyone has sinned; we all fall short of your glorious standard. Yet you, in your grace, freely make us right in your sight. You did this to demonstrate your righteousness, for you yourself are fair and just, and you make sinners right in your sight when they believe in Jesus.

ROMANS 3:23-24, 26

Once you've formed an opinion about someone, it's difficult to change it. That's why God warns us to be careful about judging others. Ask the Holy Spirit to reveal anyone you've been judging in your heart. Do you really know that person's story? How would you want to be treated?

WHAT IS AT THE HEART OF YOUR AMBITIONS?

Lord, how can I know if my ambitions are healthy or unhealthy?

When you follow the desires of your sinful nature, the results are very clear: sexual immorality, impurity, lustful pleasures, idolatry, sorcery, hostility, quarreling, jealousy, outbursts of anger, selfish ambition, dissension, division, envy. A tree is identified by its fruit. Figs are never gathered from thornbushes, and grapes are not picked from bramble bushes. A good person produces good things from the treasury of a good heart, and an evil person produces evil things from the treasury of an evil heart.

GALATIANS 5:19-21; LUKE 6:44-45

Is it possible to be an ambitious believer?

Since you have been raised to new life with Christ, set your sights on the realities of heaven. Whatever you do, do it all for my glory. Focus on this one thing: Forgetting the past and looking forward to what lies ahead, press on to reach the end of the race and receive the heavenly prize for which I, through Christ Jesus, am calling you.

COLOSSIANS 3:1; I CORINTHIANS 10:31; PHILIPPIANS 3:13-14

What can I pray to remind me to use my ambitions for your glory?
Let love be my highest goal! But may I also desire the special abilities the Spirit gives. Be exalted, O God, above the highest heavens. May your glory shine over all the earth. Show me where to walk, for I give myself to you. Teach me to do your will, for you are my God.

I CORINTHIANS 14:1; PSALM 108:5; PSALM 143:8, 10

Reflect on one area of ambition in your life and prayerfully ask yourself these questions: What fuels my ambition? Is it for my own recognition or for God to be recognized through me? Do I want others to admire me or to admire God? Do I seek to fulfill my desires or seek God's desires for me? Whose glory am I really seeking? If your ambition is misaligned, confess this to God, receive his gracious forgiveness, and ask him to align your desires with his.

THE LORD DIRECTS THE STEPS OF THE GODLY

Lord, what is your advice when I have
an important decision to make?

Get wisdom; develop good judgment. Don't forget
my words or turn away from them. You know what I
want; you know what is right because you have been
taught my law. I direct the steps of the godly. I delight
in every detail of their lives.

PROVERBS 4:5; ROMANS 2:18; PSALM 37:23

How will I know my decision is pleasing to you?

If you love me, obey my commandments. I have
called you to live a holy life, not an impure life.
Therefore, anyone who refuses to live by these rules is
not disobeying human teaching but is rejecting me,
who gives the Holy Spirit to you. Trust in me with
all your heart; do not depend on your own understanding. Seek my will in all you do, and I will show
you which path to take.

JOHN 14:15; 1 THESSALONIANS 4:7-8;
PROVERBS 3:5-6

What can I pray to ask you what is best?

Bend down, O LORD, and hear my prayer; answer me, for I need your help. You are the LORD my God, who teaches me what is good for me and leads me along the paths I should follow.

PSALM 86:1; ISAIAH 48:17

Spend some time this morning reflecting on the daily decisions and choices you make. Are you facing a big life decision? What outcomes would make you feel as if you made wise choices? Does pleasing the Lord factor into your decision-making process? Remember that God delights in every detail of your life. In prayer, invite God to guide your decisions, and voice your trust in his ability to guide you.

REASONS TO WORSHIP

Lord, how can I put my heart in a posture to worship you?
Never forget the good things I do for you. Cry out for
insight, and ask for understanding. Search for them as
you would for silver; seek them like hidden treasures.
Then you will understand what it means to fear me, and
you will gain knowledge of me. Worship me with gladness. Acknowledge that I am God! I made you, and you
are mine. Enter my gates with thanksgiving; go into my
courts with praise. Give thanks to me and bless my name.

PSALM 103:2; PROVERBS 2:3-5; PSALM 100:2-4

How can I specifically worship you right now?
I am worthy to receive glory and honor and power.
For I created all things, and they exist because I created what I pleased. I existed before anything else,
and I hold all creation together. I hold you by your
right hand—I, the LORD your God. And I say to you,
"Don't be afraid. I am here to help you." For I am a
merciful God; I will not abandon you.

REVELATION 4:11; COLOSSIANS 1:17;
ISAIAH 41:13; DEUTERONOMY 4:31

What can I pray as an act of worship to you?
Oh, Lord, how great are your riches and wisdom and knowledge! How impossible it is for me to understand your decisions and your ways! For who can know your thoughts? Who knows enough to give you advice? And who has given you so much that you need to pay it back? For everything comes from you and exists by your power and is intended for your glory. All glory to you forever! Amen.

ROMANS 11:33-36

In his book The Spirit of the Disciplines, *Dallas Willard writes, "In worship we engage ourselves with, dwell upon, and express the greatness, beauty, and goodness of God through . . . words, rituals, and symbols." You can do this anytime and anywhere. Take time to reflect on God's greatness described in his Word, his beauty shown in the world, and his goodness exhibited in your life. Respond to him with praise, thanksgiving, and worship.*

WHY GOD MAKES PROMISES

Lord, how do you back up your promises?
By my divine power, I have given you everything you need for living a godly life. You have received all of this by coming to know me. And because of my glory and excellence, I have given you great and precious promises. These are the promises that enable you to share my divine nature and escape the world's corruption caused by human desires.

2 PETER 1:3-4

How do your promises help me grow spiritually?
In view of all this, make every effort to respond to my promises. Supplement your faith with a generous provision of moral excellence, and moral excellence with knowledge, and knowledge with self-control, and self-control with patient endurance, and patient endurance with godliness, and godliness with brotherly affection, and brotherly affection with love for everyone. The more you grow like this, the more

188

productive and useful you will be in your knowledge of me.

2 PETER 1:5-8

What can I pray to claim your promises to me?
Lord, you keep your covenant and show unfailing love to all who walk before you in wholehearted devotion.

2 CHRONICLES 6:14

God gives his promises so we can respond in trust and build practices that nourish our souls. This morning, create a spiritual practice that is your response to a promise from God. Try to practice it all day (or all week!). For example, practice daily forgiveness based on the promise in Luke 6:37: "Forgive others, and you will be forgiven." Or commit your day to the Lord with this command from Psalm 37:5: "Commit everything you do to the LORD. Trust him, and he will help you."

WHAT ARE YOU WORTH?

Lord, I often feel tempted to doubt my worth.
How do you see me?

I created human beings in my own image. Male and
female I created them. I chose to give birth to you by
giving you my true word. And you, out of all creation,
became my prized possession. You are my masterpiece.
I have created you anew in Christ Jesus, so you can do
the good things I planned for you long ago.

GENESIS 1:27; JAMES 1:18; EPHESIANS 2:10

But how am I worthy of being your
"prized possession"?

Even before I made the world, I loved you and chose
you in Christ to be holy and without fault in my
eyes. I decided in advance to adopt you into my own
family by bringing you to myself through Jesus Christ.
This is what I wanted to do, and it gave me great
pleasure.

EPHESIANS 1:4-5

What can I pray when I feel worthless?

How precious are your thoughts about me, O God.
They cannot be numbered! What are mere mortals
that you should think about us, human beings that
you care for us? You have made us a little lower than
yourself and crowned us with glory and honor.

PSALM 139:17; PSALM 8:4-5

God doesn't base your worth on your appearance or accomplishments. He sees you as worthy because he created you in his image, adopted you into his family, and loves you as his child. Think of a statement that can anchor you in the truth of your worth. For example, "I am a child of God" or "My heavenly Father calls me his prized possession." Enter this statement in your phone and have it pop up every morning as a daily reminder of your great worth in God's eyes.

GOD CAN USE YOU, FLAWS AND ALL

Lord, how can you work through me even though I don't feel qualified?

My grace is all you need. My power works best in weakness. I know those who are mine, and all who belong to me must turn away from evil. If you keep yourself pure, you will be a special utensil for honorable use. Your life will be clean, and you will be ready for me to use you for every good work.

2 CORINTHIANS 12:9; 2 TIMOTHY 2:19, 21

What examples from your Word show how you work through ordinary people?

Moses pleaded, "O Lord, I'm not very good with words. I never have been, and I'm not now, even though you have spoken to me. I get tongue-tied, and my words get tangled." Then I asked Moses, "Who makes a person's mouth? Is it not I, the LORD? I will be with you as you speak, and I will instruct you in what to say."

EXODUS 4:10-12

*What can I pray when I feel unworthy
to be used by you?*

I pray that from your glorious, unlimited resources
you will empower me with inner strength through
your Spirit. Now all glory to you, God, who are able,
through your mighty power at work within me, to
accomplish infinitely more than I might ask or think.

EPHESIANS 3:16, 20

*Moses wasn't an eloquent speaker, yet God used him to lead the Israelites
out of Egypt. What sins or flaws make you feel unusable by God? You are
qualified because (1) you are a child of God, created in his image; (2) he has
given you his grace; and (3) you desire to be used by him. Pray the above
prayer again. Thank God that he doesn't expect you to struggle on your own,
but that he empowers you with his unlimited resources.*

DON'T LET REGRET
DEFEAT YOU

*Lord, can regret over past mistakes
ever be a good thing?*
The kind of sorrow I want you to experience leads
you away from sin and results in salvation. There's no
regret for that kind of sorrow.

2 CORINTHIANS 7:10

What is an example of heartfelt regret over sin?
Ezra fell to his knees and lifted his hands to me. He
prayed, "O my God, I am utterly ashamed; I blush
to lift up my face to you. For our sins are piled
higher than our heads, and our guilt has reached to
the heavens. From the days of our ancestors until
now, we have been steeped in sin. O LORD, God of
Israel, you are just. We come before you in our guilt,
though in such a condition none of us can stand in
your presence."

EZRA 9:5-7, 15

What can I pray to turn regret into renewal?
Those who look to you for help, Lord, will be radiant
with joy; no shadow of shame will darken our faces.

PSALM 34:5

Recall a moment of regret when you had really messed up. What feelings accompany this memory? Shame? Embarrassment? Sometimes those memories can be divine moments where God meets you in your regret and uses it to turn your life in a new direction. You are not meant to stay stuck in remorse. Confess it to the Lord and ask for his forgiveness. Begin your prayer with your hands over your face; then remove your hands as a symbol that the shadow of shame is no longer with you.

REWARDS AWAIT YOU

Lord, will you reward me for how I've lived my life?
Anyone who wants to come to me must believe that
I exist and that I reward those who sincerely seek me.
But on the judgment day, fire will reveal what kind
of work each builder has done. The fire will show if
a person's work has any value. If the work survives,
that builder will receive a reward.

HEBREWS 11:6; 1 CORINTHIANS 3:13-14

*How can I stay focused on eternal rewards despite
the sacrifices involved?*
Everyone who has given up houses or brothers or sisters or father or mother or children or property, for my
sake, will receive a hundred times as much in return
and will inherit eternal life. Give, and you will receive.
Your gift will return to you in full—pressed down,
shaken together to make room for more, running over,
and poured into your lap. The amount you give will
determine the amount you get back.

MATTHEW 19:29; LUKE 6:38

What prayer can help me focus on heavenly rewards?

Whether I am here in this body or away from this body, my goal is to please you, Lord. For we must all stand before Christ to be judged. I will receive whatever I deserve for the good or evil I have done in this earthly body.

2 CORINTHIANS 5:9-10

Start an "eternal investment" savings jar with whatever change or bills you have in your wallet, with a goal to save twenty-five, fifty, or one hundred dollars. Periodically add a few dollars to the jar until you reach your goal. Then give that money away. Ask the Holy Spirit to guide your gift to the right person or organization. Use this exercise to remind you that your work to serve God and others here on earth is storing up rewards in heaven.

THE BLESSINGS OF BELONGING TO GOD

Lord, what are the privileges of belonging to you?
I have blessed you with every spiritual blessing in the heavenly realms because you are united with Christ. Now you are no longer a slave but my own child. And since you are my child, I have made you my heir. There is no condemnation for you who belong to Christ Jesus. For you are a holy people, who belong to me. I have chosen you to be my own special treasure.

EPHESIANS 1:3; GALATIANS 4:7; ROMANS 8:1; DEUTERONOMY 7:6

Lord Jesus, how do these privileges influence the way I live?
When you obey my commandments, you remain in my love, just as I obey my Father's commandments and remain in his love. This is my commandment: Love each other in the same way I have loved you. There is no greater love than to lay down one's life for one's friends. You are my friends if you do what

I command. I no longer call you slaves, because a master doesn't confide in his slaves. Now you are my friends, since I have told you everything the Father told me.

JOHN 15:10, 12-15

What can I pray to thank you for accepting me?
Anyone who belongs to Christ has become a new person. The old life is gone; a new life has begun! And all of this is a gift from you, God, who brought me back to yourself through Christ.

2 CORINTHIANS 5:17-18

God's acceptance frees you to offer others the same loving acceptance. Today, ask yourself who in your life needs an invitation to belong. Invite someone over for dinner so he or she can feel a sense of belonging. As you set an extra place at the table, thank God for how he's made space for you at his table.

STAND IN AWE

*Lord, how can I recapture a sense of
amazement about you?*

I am the everlasting God, the Creator of all the earth.
The heavens proclaim my glory. The skies display
my craftsmanship. The highest heavens and the earth
and everything in it all belong to me. For I am the
God of gods and Lord of lords. I am the great God,
the mighty and awesome God. At the right time I
will bring everything together under the authority
of Christ—everything in heaven and on earth.

ISAIAH 40:28; PSALM 19:1; DEUTERONOMY 10:14, 17;
EPHESIANS 1:10

*Lord, how can I live in a way that gives you
the glory you deserve?*

What do I require of you? I require only that you fear
me, and live in a way that pleases me, and love me
and serve me with all your heart and soul. And you
must always obey my commands and decrees that I
am giving you today for your own good.

DEUTERONOMY 10:12-13

*What can I pray as I reflect on your
amazing work in creation?*

Lord, let the heavens be glad, and the earth rejoice!
Let the sea and everything in it shout your praise!
Let the fields and their crops burst out with joy! Let
the trees of the forest sing for joy before you, LORD,
for you are coming! You are coming to judge the
earth. You will judge the world with justice, and
the nations with your truth.

PSALM 96:11-13

*God's amazing work is everywhere—from speaking the heavens and earth
into existence, to quiet miracles like a beautiful sunset or the faithful beating of
your heart. The more you look for evidence of God's work, the more amazed
you will be. Try to watch the sunset today or catch tomorrow's sunrise. Try to
soak in the miracle of it—only an amazing God could create such splendor.*

BOLDNESS IN THE FACE OF OPPOSITION

What is an example from Scripture of someone who showed bold faith in the face of opposition?

Then Peter, filled with the Holy Spirit, said, "There is salvation in no one else! God has given no other name under heaven by which we must be saved." The members of the council were amazed when they saw the boldness of Peter and John, for they could see that they were ordinary men with no special training in the Scriptures. They also recognized them as men who had been with Jesus.

ACTS 4:8, 12-13

How will you help me when I feel intimidated?

Since you have a great High Priest who has entered heaven, Jesus my Son, hold firmly to what you believe. This High Priest of yours understands your weaknesses, for he faced all of the same testings you do, yet he did not sin. So come boldly to my throne.

There you will receive my mercy, and you will find grace to help you when you need it most.

HEBREWS 4:14-16

*What can I pray when I need courage
to speak up for you?*
O Lord, hear their threats, and give me, your servant, great boldness in preaching your word. Stretch out your hand with healing power; may miraculous signs and wonders be done through the name of your holy servant Jesus.

ACTS 4:29-30

The believers in the early church didn't pray for God to remove their hardships. Instead, they asked God to help them be bold despite their hardships. So often we want God to take away our struggles, but God can use times of testing to deepen our faith and use us to witness to those around us. Are you going through a difficult season right now? Ask the Lord to give you the courage to be a bold witness for him.

GOD KNOWS YOUR
REAL MOTIVES

Lord, how can I live with purer motives?
Seek my Kingdom above all else, and live righteously.
People may be pure in their own eyes, but I examine
their motives. I search all hearts and examine secret
motives. I give all people their due rewards, according
to what their actions deserve.

MATTHEW 6:33; PROVERBS 16:2; JEREMIAH 17:10

What are some signs that I am acting
with the wrong motives?
Don't be selfish; don't try to impress others. Don't
do your good deeds publicly, to be admired by
others. Give your gifts in private. When you pray,
don't be like the hypocrites who love to pray publicly where everyone can see them. When you pray,
go away by yourself, shut the door behind you, and
pray to me in private. Then I, who see everything,
will reward you.

PHILIPPIANS 2:3; MATTHEW 6:1, 4-6

*How can I prayerfully ask you to point out
my misguided motives?*

Put me on trial, LORD, and cross-examine me. Test my
motives and my heart.

PSALM 26:2

*We must be willing to allow God to search and examine our motives and
point out where we aren't completely sincere. Ask him where your motives
might not be fully honest. Are there areas of selfish ambition? Was an act of
kindness done just to make you look good, or did you truly want to help? Do
you ever try to bargain with God or manipulate him in prayer to promote
your kingdom over his? Confess impure motives to God so that he can help
your actions come from a pure heart of service to him.*

Notes

1. Lewis B. Smedes, *Forgive and Forget: Healing the Hurts We Don't Deserve* (New York: HarperCollins, 1996), 133.
2. C. S. Lewis, *Mere Christianity* (New York: HarperOne, 2001), 128.
3. Dallas Willard, *The Spirit of the Disciplines: Understanding How God Changes Lives* (New York: HarperCollins, 1988), 177.